FORCES OF HORDES

CIRCLE ORBOROS

CREDITS

HORDES created by
Matt Wilson

Project Director
Bryan Cutler

Game Design
Matt Wilson

Lead Designer
Jason Soles

Additional Development
David Carl
Brian Putnam

Art Direction
Kris Aubin

Lead Writer
Douglas Seacat

Additional Writing
Simon Berman
David Carl
Matt DiPietro
Ron Kruzie
Aeryn Rudel
Jason Soles
Matt Wilson

Continuity
Jason Soles

Editing
Darla Kennerud
Sheelin Arnaud

Cover Illustration
Andrea Uderzo

Illustrations
Andrew Arconti
Carlos Cabrera
Eric Deschamps
Matt Dixon
Emrah Elmasli
Adam Gillespie
Imaginary Friends Studios
Andrea Uderzo
Brian Valenzuela
Chris Walton
Matt Wilson
Kieran Yanner

Concept Illustration
Roberto Cirillo
Joshua McDowell
Chris Walton
Matt Wilson

Graphic Design & Layout
Kris Aubin
Kim Goddard
Josh Manderville
Stuart Spengler

Studio Director
Ron Kruzie

Miniature Sculpting
Sean Bullogh
Greg Clavilier
Benoit Cosse
Jeff Grace
Todd Harris
Jason Hendricks
Werner Klocke
Oliver Nkweti Lafitte
Aragorn Marks
Jerzy Montwill
Paul Muller
Stefan Nieheus
Edgar Ramos
Jose Roig
Ben Saunders
Steve Saunders
Kev White
Jeff Wilhelm

Resin Caster
Sean Bullough

Miniature Painting
Matt DiPietro
Ron Kruzie
Allison McVey
Quentin Smith

Hobby Manager
Rob Hawkins

Terrain
Alfonzo Falco
Rob Hawkins

Photography
Kris Aubin
Rob Hawkins

Development Manager
David Carl

President
Sherry Yeary

Chief Creative Officer
Matt Wilson

Creative Director
Ed Bourelle

Executive Assistant
Chare Kerzman

Project Manager
Shona Fahland

Marketing Coordinator
William Shick

Retail Support and Development
Ross Thompson

Customer Service
Adam Johnson

Events Coordinator
Jason Martin

Community Manager & Staff Writer
Simon Berman

Volunteer Coordinator
Jen Ikuta

No Quarter EIC
Aeryn Rudel

Licensing & Contract Manager
Brent Waldher

Production Director
Mark Christensen

Technical Director
Kelly Yeager

Production Manager
Doug Colton

Production
Trey Alley
Max Barsana
Victoria Boldt
Alex Chobot

Jack Coleman
Cody Ellis
Joel Falkenhagen
Joe Lee
Michael McIntosh
Nick Scherdnik
Jacob Stanley
Benjamin Tracy

Sys Admin/Webmaster
Chris Ross

Infernals
Jeremy Galeone
Peter Gaublomme
Joachim Molkow
Brian Putnam
Gilles Reynaud
Donald Sullivan

Playtest Coordinator
David Carl

Internal Playtesters
Simon Berman
Ed Bourelle
David Carl
Jack Coleman
Bryan Cutler
Dave Dauterive
Michael Faciane
Ben Misenar
Douglas Seacat
William Shick
Jason Soles
Brent Waldher
Chris Walton

External Playtesters
Alex Badion
Our Player Community
Mike Emery
Eric Ernewein
Steve Fortson
Nick Kendall
Rob Miles
Field Test Participants
Josh Saulter
John Simon
Tim Simpson
Mark Thomas
Anthony Woods

Proofreading
Darla Kennerud
Aeryn Rudel
William Shick
Brent Waldher

THE POWER OF STONE AND STORM

FACTION BACKGROUND

Arguably humanity's most ancient organization, the Circle Orboros predates all the civilizations presently dominating western Immoren. For millennia, these powerful mystics have gathered in secret to master the energies of nature and wield that power as a versatile tool and formidable weapon. The entity they call Orboros manifests in raging storms, blazing lightning, roaring thunder, unrelenting floods, and the consuming hunger of wild beasts. Druids of the Circle call on these primal forces and bend them to their will.

The Circle Orboros has stepped from the fringes to join battle against enemies who would despoil their sacred sites or whose mere existence defiles Orboros. The druids extend their will through a large group of loosely organized warriors called the Wolves of Orboros as well as through the tribal and bloodthirsty Tharn.

At the beck and call of the druids and their allies are great beasts of the wilds, including savage warpwolves, powerful satyrs, enraged gorax, and other fierce creatures. Living beasts are joined by great wolds, stone-and-wood constructs brought to life by ancient ritual. Be they flesh and blood or stone and timber, these towering weapons of war stand equal to the warjacks created by the armies of the "civilized" nations.

PLAYING CIRCLE

The Circle Orboros army excels at guerilla warfare. The number of models/units capable of maneuvering terrain with ease is staggering, and Circle spells, animi, or abilities can help the few others. Some Circle models can even simply teleport to new locations, ignoring intervening models as well as terrain. Abilities like Hunter and Treewalker give Circle units a massive advantage in forest terrain, and others like Fertilizer and Forest Growth allow the Circle to create forests on command.

Beyond their mastery of nature, the ancient magic of the Circle makes them a powerful arcane army. Druid models/units have plentiful spell options, and even some Circle warbeasts can extend druidic powers across the battlefield. In addition to their magical prowess, the Circle can punish enemy magic-users for dabbling in the arts or ward entire portions of their forces from enemy spells. With a vast array of forest-dwelling warriors and some of the most powerful spellcasters in western Immoren, you can . . .

**Unleash the Wrath of Nature
on the Foes of Orboros!**

TABLE OF CONTENTS

PRIVATEER PRESS™

Visit: www.privateerpress.com

Privateer Press, Inc. 13434 NE 16th St. Suite 120 • Bellevue, WA 98005
Tel (425) 643-5900 • Fax (425) 643-5902

For online customer service, email frontdesk@privateerpress.com

Forces of HORDES: Circle Orboros . . . . ISBN: 978-1-933362-74-8 . . . . . . PIP 1041

Forces of HORDES: Circle Orboros Hardcover . . . . ISBN: 978-1-933362-75-5 . . . . . . PIP 1042

A dry, searing wind picked up the fine sand of the dunes to send it scraping across the exposed flesh of the long line of armored spearmen and crossbowmen. They were a larger gathering of Wolves of Orboros than had been collected in one place as far back as any of them could remember. Krueger the Stormlord marched near the front of the column accompanied by a pair of towering woldwardens, their granite footfalls unhindered by the sands. Amid the forward column were several other beasts bound to his will, some directed by subordinate overseers.

The energy of Orboros had its own quality in each climate. Krueger had never understood his former master's ascetic enjoyment of these arid wastes; the flows of energy coursing beneath the sands were abrasive, bitter, and unforgiving. They did not sustain him with the same vitality he felt in the high mountain peaks amid the rumble of thunder and torrential downpours.

Krueger sensed an unusual perturbation in the invisible energy flows beneath his feet, and a wayfarer appeared ahead of the column in a swirl of dust. When the newcomer removed the black cloth covering most of his face, Krueger saw the scarred face of a personal messenger of Omnipotent Dahlekov, Senior Wayfarer Tal. The wayfarer spoke imperiously. "Krueger the Stormwrath. I bear an urgent message from the omnipotents. Will you listen?"

The column came to a gradual halt behind Krueger after he stopped. "Wayfarer Tal, speak." Even when Krueger had been on better terms with Dahlekov, he had loathed this pompous emissary.

The man drew himself up and answered loudly enough to be heard by those at the fore of the column. "Potent Krueger the Stormwrath, you are summoned to a Grand Convocation Tribunal, to convene immediately. You stand accused of fomenting insurrection and turning traitor on the order after defying the omnipotents and refusing all ordinary methods of reconciliation."

Scowling, Krueger made a dismissive noise. Tal's lip curled into a disdainful sneer as he continued. "Return with me to the tribunal to claim your right to answer the charges and plead mercy."

A flicker of white crackled across the haft of Krueger's spear and sent sparks through the steel tines. Tal's eyes widened. Krueger asked, "Do you intend to force the issue?"

Despite the fear in Tal's eyes, his tone remained haughty. "Return of your own volition, or not at all. The tribunal will proceed with or without you."

Krueger's smile was sardonic. "I'm sure you can see I have more important matters to address. Tell your masters they will have to take this matter up with me at a better time." He waved a hand dismissively.

Tal glowered. There was a crackle of distant thunder as he vanished. The Stormlord immediately signaled his army onward. The woldwardens were first to lurch into motion, the wooden beams connecting their stones creaking, and the rest of the army followed.

It had been weeks earlier when Wurmwood, the Tree of Fate, had set Krueger on the course that would lead him into the desert wastes. While the Stormlord's soldiers recuperated from recent successes against a Cryxian outpost in the southern Wyrmwall, Krueger left them to locate that mysterious tree, taking only Wolf Lord Morraig as companion. Krueger took only two lesser wolds—a woldwyrd and a woldwatcher—against unforeseen complications.

The Tree of Fate was a close ally of the Circle Orboros, bound by ancient pacts that stretched back to the first mystics who had called themselves omnipotents. As a living repository of millennia of history and lore, it had access to the inner secrets of the order.

There was a special connection between the Tree of Fate and devoted priests of the Devourer, who received periodic visions drawing them to it. The tree never stayed in one place long, vanishing without warning to reappear thousands of miles away. Only its cultists knew where to go to offer bloody sacrifices upon the soil above its roots. Krueger had wrung clues to the tree's likely location from several; the descriptions were dreamlike and vague, but he recognized commonalities that told him where to search.

Krueger collected his wolds and the wolf lord and they went to the Shattered Teeth site after nightfall. It was an ancient stone ring hidden within a forested glade halfway up Mount Garsor in the Wyrmwall, a strong node locus. The attending keeper eyed him and the wolf lord with clear apprehension but deferred to his authority and enacted the chanted rites to initiate the passage. The circle of stones came alive with pulsing green light. Krueger felt a familiar itching across his skin and pressure like his weight being magnified tenfold as the earth seized him. Riding in his wake, Wolf Lord Morraig and his wolds were like anchors dragging him down and sapping his mystical strength.

There was the typical shock to his system as his environment changed. The thin, cold air, redolent with pine and bark, was suddenly hot and humid, tinged with the earthy smell of a nearby riverbank. The rain-soaked wood had become dry brush and sage.

This site was north of Lake Scarleforth, ground recently won back from trollkin kriels. Krueger took his bearings and committed to a lengthy hike into the formidable mountains serving as the southern barrier of the shrouded nation of Ios. The wolf lord and Krueger conversed little during the journey, but as they topped a rise toward the higher passes, Morraig's curiosity prompted him to speak. "Why not await Kromac's return to bring him, Stormlord? I know little of this Wurmwood, neither how to address it nor show it respect."

Krueger eyed the red-headed warrior astride his armored wolf. "Your indifference to spiritual matters suits me. I sent the Tharn away deliberately." The wolf lord grunted in surprise, prompting a chuckle from Krueger. "Kromac's errand against the trollkin is important to consolidating my power in the southern Wyrmwall, but I did not want him here regardless. Wurmwood's support would rally the cultists as never before, particularly the Tharn. Yet I must prepare for any eventuality."

Morraig's eyes narrowed with sudden understanding. "If the Tree of Fate turns on you, the Tharn may take it badly."

Krueger's smile was thin, and he inclined his head slightly. "Your own loyalties are not based on religious impulses, which I appreciate."

They topped the intended rise just as the sun began to descend below the horizon. Twisted rock formations loomed above them like gnarled fingers of stone, just as described from the dreams of the cultists. Stepping onto the broad bluff revealed a spectacular view. The ground sloped slightly downward toward a sheer cliff descending to the Bloodstone Marches, which extended to the horizon. Directly southwest lay Scarleforth Lake, gleaming like pooled blood in the light of the setting sun.

A dark cave yawned in the mountain wall; beyond it, directly adjacent to the cliff's edge, was the rooted form of Wurmwood. The setting sun cast its leafless and rune-scarred trunk into sharp relief where the bark was scraped to allow for runic whorls of ancient druidic power, and its hoary roots spilled out over the rocky ground. Grisly trophies adorned the tree, from bones tied into its branches to a larger collection of skulls collected among the niches in its trunk.

They had hardly stepped forward before two stone columns flanking their path flared to life with a glow of green runes. A half-dozen collections of scrap wood and sharpened twigs assembled themselves into loosely man-shaped forms. Their wooden frames quivered with eagerness to attack. Morraig cursed and drew his snarling wolf up short. The woldwatcher stepped swiftly near the Stormlord, ready to interpose itself, while a gleam of power gathered within the crystal focusing orb at the center of the woldwyrd.

Krueger halted and called out, "Wurmwood! I bring a proposal—" He realized his mistake even as the words came. His mind had been preoccupied. Not seeing Cassius had prompted him to address Wurmwood directly, a severe violation of the etiquette. He must speak to the conduit, feigning discourse of one druid to another.

The arms of the mannikins exploded in flesh-shredding sprays of deadly splinters. The woldwatcher leapt in front of Krueger to absorb the wooden shrapnel, while Morraig raised his shield and his wolf crouched and turned its head away to allow its armored neck plates to take the brunt.

Morraig and his wolf bounded forward to retaliate. The wolf shouldered through one mannikin and bit through a second even as its rider's sword clove through a third. Krueger pointed his spear, and the air split as a lightning bolt shattered the nearest one. The floating woldwyrd behind him eliminated the remaining two with a pair of energy bolts fired from its crystal oculus. The animated constructs were not the real threat, being simply extensions of the sentry stones, but Krueger had no intention of escalating the conflict.

He saw Cassius the Oathkeeper at last, in the center of the bluff with one of Wurmwood's roots encircling his hooded and robed form. Tremendously gaunt, he held in one hand the cleft sword Genesis. His expression was baleful, and something ancient peered through those eyes. Thick-bodied warriors bearing axes rushed from the cave near Wurmwood. They had the distinctly lupine heads of skinwalkers, with bestial faces. A section of rune-laden mountain wall near the cave broke free and revealed itself to be a wold guardian, which strode toward the intruders.

Krueger let the winds lift him into the air. "Hold, Cassius!" At the name, some remnant of human expression touched the face of the tree's conduit. "I am Krueger the Stormlord. We are allies!"

Cassius raised a hand toward his warriors. The skinwalkers growled and were answered by Morraig's mount, but they stopped their advance.

The druid had been chosen as Oathkeeper fifty years ago, while he was a youthful wilder. Whatever his life might have become had been erased when his mind was scraped clean for the tree. Only glimmers of a person remained in the conduit whose fleshy brain Wurmwood required to interact with mortals. The tree was an alien creature with a mind unlike any man or beast. Within its bark lay thousands of years of rings, each touched by the primal energies of the Devourer Wurm. Its appetite for flesh was insatiable; it sustained itself through its roots, drinking both spilled blood and the very essence of Orboros.

After a long silence, Cassius spoke. "I did not call for you. Those not invited *trespass*. Trespassers tithe in blood and souls." Cassius stood directly between Krueger and Wurmwood, with the ancient wold guardian at his side.

"I am no trespasser. I come to offer a greater tithe than any number of your followers could deliver. All I ask is that you add your strength and power to mine in the months ahead. In exchange, you will feast on carnage. Every kill by every spear, every axe, every blade in my army, I offer in your name. Peer into the future and you will see the tide of blood I bring."

Cassius stared at him with fixed intensity. A sudden change in atmospheric pressure rippled, and thunder rumbled in the distance across the blood-red sands. Cassius' eyes sharpened. "There is another matter. Its solution would appease me."

Krueger drifted to the ground and leaned upon his spear. He cautiously allowed, "I will hear your conditions."

The root attached to the green-robed druid extended, pushing aside rock and dirt as it brought Cassius closer to the edge of the cliff. Krueger followed. Cassius waved his blade out over the darkening expanse. "I have recently become aware that to the southeast, the children of our ancient foe meddle with something they should not." A flash of lightning struck on the distant horizon. As it lit upon Krueger's eyes he was overtaken by a vision. He saw a massive refinery freshly built by the Protectorate of Menoth outside their borders. Its buildings seemed hastily built and still under construction, yet its machinery churned. An impressive army guarded its perimeter in temporary encampments that centered on a massive and ornate tent emblazoned with golden Menofixes and the symbol of the Temple Flameguard. At least a dozen warjacks were evident, suggesting the presence of at least one warcaster.

Cassius spoke again as this vision faded. "This is the site of a primary fulcrum convergence, one buried deep beneath the sands. Your order has never constructed a node there because the ground is unstable and the ley lines are too deep. It is a hub for the entire desert, vital to Orboros. The Menites seek to siphon their flammable oils from a massive repository adjacent to the fulcrum. Lines of fate suggest a looming disaster. If this repository ignites, it would forever alter the flow of Orboros through the desert."

Krueger considered this, feeling increased respect for the scope of Wurmwood's awareness. Omnipotents had the means to commune with the entire ley line network within their dominions, yet it seemed the Tree of Fate exceeded this. "Do you have a plan of action? Have you informed Mohsar? It is his dominion."

Cassius turned to face him, his expression showing something akin to annoyance. "Mohsar is of no consequence here. You are the one who came to meet this need."

Krueger scowled and bit back a remark regarding this reaction after the earlier attack upon him. "Our strength does not rest in direct attack, not against the armies of mankind. There must be another way. If I were not here today, what would you have done?"

"I would have intervened personally, and failed. You may yet fail as well. There is little time. Disaster looms on Calder's next full moon." The conduit spoke the words with unnerving calm. "Before you arrived, disaster was certain. Now, there is a chance."

Krueger ran through the scenario in his mind. Attacking a Menite army on their own ground was foolish, and the barren lands around the refinery offered few opportunities to exploit their tactical strengths. He could lose everything he had worked to build. "I am not the one for this. Mohsar should be told."

Cassius' eyes bored into his, unblinking. "Mohsar is occupied. Your brethren have ever been slow to respond to the call to war. The omnipotents could not muster an adequate force in time. You alone can do this: your army stands ready."

"The world regularly suffers ills we cannot fix."

Cassius looked away. "This will critically destabilize the eastern dominion, which already suffers a widening wound opened by the skorne. A matter Mohsar has failed to correct."

Krueger felt the weight of that. His schemes would be impossible if the Circle suffered such a dramatic reduction in power. He gritted his teeth. "If I accomplish this, you will support my efforts?"

Once again Wurmwood's conduit was silent for a long time before responding. "It is agreed." The words resonated with power, as if they were now written in the immortal rings of the Tree of Fate. "Gather your allies. A way will be opened."

After hastening to return to the army, Krueger and Morraig stirred them into motion. Krueger ordered his ranking leaders to proceed on the narrow mountain passes to the Broken Teeth site. He took a powerful assortment of wolds and warpwolves—most of his remaining beasts.

Dozens of senior wayfarers and keepers had assembled at the transport site, bringing a wide ring of ancillary shifting stones to bolster the shared rites. The almost perfectly triangular arrangement of the moons Calder, Laris, and Artis indicated the subterranean energies would be at high tide.

These nodes were intended for smaller groups, and Krueger and his overseers loaned their strength to the rites. They sent groups of soldiers onward through smaller jumps to other major conjunctions, the druids following to repeat the rites at each interval. It was a tremendous act of coordination that suggested Wurmwood had far more overt influence than Krueger would have suspected.

Their exit site in the Bloodstone Marches left them still at a distance from their destination, but the efforts had saved tremendous time. There was nothing more they could do except march into the desert. They traveled at night and stopped for little besides shelter. The only meaningful interruption was Wayfarer Tal's unexpected arrival with the tribunal summons, after which he was sent away empty-handed.

Tal returned immediately to his master. Dahlekov was situated near the grand conclave site, past a short walk along the lakeshore to the mountain wall. A small set of natural caverns penetrated the stone. The warpwolf stalkers guarding the cavern entrance did not flinch as Tal strode past.

Omnipotent Dahlekov waited within the largest chamber, seated in meditation before a low-banked, smoky fire that sent choking black ash up to the ceiling and made the air close and stifling. Little of the omnipotent's black robes and bronzed druidic armor conveyed his rank, but he exuded awareness and latent power. "Krueger did not come."

Tal dropped to one knee. "He refused, Omnipotent. He mocked the authority of the convocation!"

Dahlekov grunted. "I thought he might, and this works to our favor. While the tribunal is underway, maintain a discreet watch upon him. When you receive my signal, you will make your move, as we discussed."

Tal's eyes darted to either side before he spoke, although there was no one to overhear. "I am honored to have your trust, Omnipotent. Still, I worry whether I will be sufficient to the task . . ."

Dahlekov considered this. "Your fears are understandable. Krueger is your superior in almost every regard." He did not seem concerned that his subordinate flinched at this. "Yet he is reckless. Where he goes, there will be battle, and he will imperil himself. All you must do is choose your moment. Await my order. It would be unseemly were he to expire before the tribunal reached its decision. Go."

The wayfarer bowed deeply before rising to depart.

The site chosen for the Grand Conclave Tribunal was along the northern shore of a small, mystically potent lake high amid the northern Wyrmwall Mountains. Two great cairns were stacked along the shore. Between these a flat piece of stone extended into the water, supporting a massive square of ancient basalt serving as an altar. This had been the site for countless sacrifices in old times and was still occasionally used for special rites requiring blood spilled under the open stars.

The three omnipotents waited atop the raised stone at the near end with the altar behind them. Mohsar the Desertwalker stood at the center in the position of seniority. He was the smallest and most aged of the three, his face shadowed by the hood of his yellow robe. In this last hour before twilight the sun found him and shone down with unnatural intensity through intervening clouds. At his right was Dahlekov the Scourging Wind, twice the bulk of Mohsar, with a square frame covered in thickly layered black robes and bronzed armor. Lortus the Watcher stood to Mohsar's left, as tall as Dahlekov but slender, his face defined by sharp angles. His head was bare, and around his neck a golden torc terminating in serpent heads cast the black web of blighted scar tissue along his neck and cheek into sharp relief.

> ## "THE MATTER AT HAND IS AN ACCUSATION OF FOMENTING INSURRECTION AND TURNING TRAITOR."

Assembled in a loose semicircle facing the omnipotents were the rest of the order's potents. It had been quite some time since a grand conclave, as the order was occupied with conflicts abroad. The expectant air was augmented both by the awareness of the significance of the tribunal and the fact that each of them had urgent tasks pending. Only Morvahna the Autumnblade seemed at ease.

Mohsar's voice carried over the gathering. "Let this tribunal commence. The matter at hand is an accusation of fomenting insurrection and turning traitor, levied against the potent Krueger the Stormwrath. Is the accused present?"

Dahlekov answered, "The accused was formally notified of these proceedings. He refused to accompany my messenger and thus surrenders the right to speak in his defense."

Mohsar's expression was stony. "Are all members of the grand convocation present?"

Lortus spoke this time. "All are present excepting the accused and Baldur the Stonecleaver. His . . . condition . . . exempts him from attendance. We may proceed."

Mohsar grumbled, "We should simply record him as deceased and move on. His territories should be reallocated."

Lortus shook his head. "That is a matter for another time."

Mohsar made a dismissive noise. "Very well. His absence will not inhibit our decisions. The penalty for traitors is death. Will the accuser step forward?" Dahlekov cleared his throat and took a step toward the center, sharing a brief look with Morvahna, whose lips were touched with a cruel smile.

What worried Krueger was how exposed they would be on their approach to the drilling and refinery buildings. The recently built Protectorate facility comprised three large structures connected by a variety of heavy pipes, along with a number of inconsequential outbuildings. From the descriptions of the scouting reeves, Krueger determined the two larger outer buildings on the extreme north and south must be the drilling and pumping stations, equipped with heavy steam-driven machinery to reach the underground deposits of oil and siphon it forth. The extracted substance passed through thick pipes into the much larger central facility to be processed.

As they neared, Krueger began to sense flows of tremendous power converging far below the sands from five different directions. Even the small taste of it from the surface was heady. He could not directly connect to them, though. Without the proper sequenced stones to draw their energy to the surface, they were like the oil deposits the Menites sought, trapped far below, and he without proper drill or pipes to harness them.

A shout from the reeves caught his attention, and he saw several race off toward the nearest adjacent dune to the left of the column, bringing their double crossbows to bear. Following them were the sleek floating forms of woldstalkers, guided by their stoneward. What had caught their attention were several hunched forms atop the dune ridge. Krueger pulled on the wind to lend speed to his motion and hastened to the top of the ridge for a better view, seeing Idrian tribesmen with rifles. Several fired upon the reeves and stalkers even as crossbow bolts flew in their direction. The tribal riflemen tumbled back over the other side of the dune to flee.

Wolf Lord Morraig had come forward and cursed under his breath. "Idrian scouts, likely in the Protectorate's employ."

Krueger frowned. "Don't let them escape."

The lord of the Wolves gave a cry, and his thick-shouldered mount surged forward at speed. He raised his sword in a circular motion, signaling their handlers to set loose the war wolves. The animals rapidly outpaced their two-legged counterparts.

Several of the Idrians turned and fired at the war wolves, taking one down before the others were upon them. The wily scout at the fore managed to set alight an oil-soaked torch that emitted profuse smoke and hurl it high into the air even as Morraig closed on him and cut him down with his sword. Krueger had no doubt both the lit brand and the gouts of oily smoke were visible from quite a distance. The damage was done.

Krueger swiftly returned to the column, shouting orders to the chieftains. He collected a group of veterans to accompany him and several of his warbeasts and headed the group out at double time, knowing the enemy would now be forewarned.

When Morraig rode up alongside, Krueger said, "We must strike immediately. We'll take a vanguard force against the drilling platform atop the southern hill first. We can defend the higher ground against any counterattack."

Morraig nodded sharply. "Where do you need me?"

"In the vanguard with me," Krueger affirmed. Reacting to his mental summons, his wolds and warpwolves rushed forward. "Have your most trusted chieftains advance the army directly toward the central building. I want them visible and closing on the enemy garrison by the time we attack the hill. They are *not* to engage in a mass assault. Order them to skirmish and retreat. Harass the enemy, but minimize our casualties."

Such orders were in keeping with the Wolves' preferred tactics, but Krueger felt the need to be explicit. The more zealous Devourer cultists knew they faced an army of Menites, and the enmity between their faiths was fierce. Krueger cared little for the individual safety of his Wolves, but he had worked too hard gathering them to waste them. More importantly, killing the Menites protecting the facility was not his goal.

Leaving Morraig to pass orders, the Stormlord and the forward segment of Wolves and reeves hastened onward. Two groups of woldstalkers also sped forward, impelled to greater speed by their controlling stonewards. Krueger left a number of his warbeasts in reserve with the army but brought two woldwardens, a pureblood and a feral warpwolf, a pair of woldwatchers, and a trio of woldwyrds. He allowed the woldwardens and woldwatchers, the slowest of these, to fall behind as he raced his army toward their destination.

When they topped the hill, for a moment Krueger believed they had taken the target entirely by surprise despite the earlier encounter with the Idrians. The squat structure loomed along the flat section of ground at the hill's apex, a profusion of hastily erected iron, wood, and stone. The mechanism it utilized to send its drill deep below the earth and draw forth the black sludge that would become Menoth's Fury was in full operation: smoke billowed from stacks above, and there was a rhythmic deep thumping that shook the entire structure.

Krueger's chosen pureblood, a beast named Graupel, growled deep in his throat and stepped forward with clenched claws. The feral followed, sniffing the wind, and the moonlight revealed a swiftly advancing line of gleaming spears and golden helmets. A sizable phalanx of Temple Flameguard marched in ordered formation around the building. From behind them came the distinct noise of ignitions and expelled gas, then rockets flew forth to explode amid the Circle's soldiers, tearing apart several Wolves.

A pair of light Protectorate warjacks escorted the Flameguard advance, each armed with pole axe and shield. A high-ranking Flameguard priest directed them from behind the block of infantry. The adorned priest pointed the soldiers onward, maintaining their line even as several in the forward rank fell to reeve crossbow bolts.

The Flameguard expertly used their heavy shields to catch most of the incoming bolts. They readied their spears, tips alight with orange fire, and lunged forward to strike the nearest Wolves. Rockets continued to pour forth and explode into the scattering Circle forces. Morraig yelled for the reeves to fall back as they fired and for the Wolves to circle around to either side, knowing they would suffer if facing the enemy line-to-line.

Krueger pointed his spear at the center of the advancing wall of shields. Green sigils circled his hand as he gathered his power to invoke a surge of lightning to explode through them. They screamed in agony and collapsed, their bodies convulsing. Krueger next summoned a great gale of wind into a raging cyclone with him at the center. It howled around him with such strength that incoming rockets spun away and fell short.

Simultaneously he latched onto the pureblood's mind and will with his own. With Krueger looking through its eyes, Graupel gave a bone-shattering howl, prompting a ripple of supernatural energy to hammer through the forward Flameguard. Armor impacted by this battery of sound cracked or buckled, while flesh tore and bones exploded into splinters. Krueger urged his woldwyrds to add their fire to send lancing beams of greenish light amid the spearmen.

The rest of the Flameguard stayed resolute as those in rear ranks moved forward to replace the fallen. Where they managed to engage the Wolves, Circle soldiers fell or were lit ablaze. Krueger could see a far larger force of soldiers down on the lower ground before the main facility, some few diverting toward the hill while most prepared to receive the main Circle army closing on them from the west.

Morraig's attempt to confound the enemy by dividing his Wolves partially succeeded as a small group slipped past the spearmen to charge the Deliverers and put an end to rockets from that quarter. Those brave Wolves were immediately set upon by Flameguard. Krueger shouted to the wolf lord, "Gather your men and pull to the left, even if it must look like a retreat!"

As the reeves and Wolves pulled back, the Flameguard surged forward to match, sensing they had broken the foe. Krueger's slower wolds had caught up with him at last and he took to the air alongside them as they moved toward the far side. Before the enemy could react to his movement, Krueger willed the woldwardens to create great eruptions of vines and spiny trees from the barren desert sands. The woldwatchers invoked their natural power to send lightning shooting from the soil beneath two of the nearest enemies, incinerating them. From their dying flesh additional trees and knotted bushes appeared, soaked in blood, creating a long line of dense foliage.

Krueger set his warpwolves on the warjacks escorting the Flameguard while his woldwardens closed on the drilling facility. Unleashing their full ferocity, the warpwolves made swift work of the light 'jacks, tearing armored plates aside with their claws and savaging the machinery within. Flameguard surrounded the beasts, stabbing with their spears. Howling in anger, the warpwolves regenerated as quickly as they could, but they were fully surrounded.

The Flameguard priest saw Krueger's advance too late. He shouted for a dozen spearmen on his unoccupied flank to intercept, but woldwatchers blocked the way. Entangling undergrowth and fast-sprouting trees sprang forth wherever their stony fists impacted flesh.

The woldwardens were supernaturally potent vessels for the blackclad's will. In a simultaneous outpouring of mystical energy, the Stormlord and the two marching stone constructs sent streams of white lightning against the drilling facility. The air split with thunder as blinding flashes lit the hillside. Arcing electricity consumed the blackened iron and sandstone of the structure while the joins of heavy piping cracked asunder. The steam engine groaned heavily, then connecting drive shafts and pistons crashed and the mechanism exploded. The great pipes leading to the central facility fell unhinged to send brackish black fluid pouring forth like the blood of the earth.

This southern drilling facility was critically compromised, a fact Krueger noted with satisfaction even though he knew the job was not done. He must also destroy the platform on the northern side of the main facility.

He felt the feral warpwolf die, torn apart by fire-emblazoned spears, but Graupel the pureblood yet lived. Wolves led by Morraig charged to attack those enemies besetting the white-furred beast. The woldwardens plunged into the fray with great stony fists, towering over the armored Menites. One rushed forward with its runes blazing green at Krueger's urging, stomping through every spearman and leaving a trail of broken bodies and crumpled armor.

The Menite priest pulled back with a small escort, clearly intending to retreat. He rushed toward the lower section of the hill, where reinforcements marched, but Krueger flew faster and closed on him. Pointing his cleft spear, Krueger unleashed first one and then a second bolt of pure lightning from within the weapon called Wurmtongue to cook the officer into charred wreckage. Krueger smiled grimly. He had been born among these zealots, and his own parents had attempted to burn him alive at the budding hints of his wilding. He always savored opportunities to eliminate Menites.

Krueger turned to the wayfarer standing close to hand. "Telvoso, bring us shifting stones and more blackclads, immediately!" The wayfarer nodded and disappeared in a flash.

With Mohsar's prompting at the conclave, Dahlekov stepped forward. He said, "I stand as accuser. Krueger the Stormwrath has shown flagrant disrespect for each member of our triumvirate. When I ordered him to return to his duties, not only did he refuse, he crept as a thief into one of my holdings and plundered a vital permanent record of our order, the Wyrmstone. This was an ancient tract of draconic prophecy deemed dangerous for unprepared minds."

Mohsar's voice was derisive. "We are not here to discuss theft, Dahlekov."

Dahlekov drew himself up, but the blind desert hermit was unaffected by his stern look. "I mention the stolen stone because it set Krueger on his ruinous course. He subsequently gathered his army, clearly bent on usurpation. He then defied Lortus' restriction against initiating contact with Blighterghast, Dragon of the Wyrmwall. Lortus can confirm." He looked to the third omnipotent, who nodded soberly.

Encouraged, Dahlekov continued, "Whatever lore Krueger related while in secret congress with Blighterghast, the repercussions for our order might be cataclysmic. Already we see Halfaug and Scaefang on the wing, come south to speak with Blighterghast for the first time in recorded history. Can there be any doubt this unprecedented movement was prompted by Krueger's rash actions? We must end his insurrection!"

Mohsar weighed this before saying without apparent emotion, "I agree with the accuser. Krueger's insubordination and recklessness cannot be left unpunished." He turned to Lortus. "What testimony do you offer regarding Krueger's defiance of your orders?"

Lortus was silent for a moment but then shook his head. "None. Rather, I would speak in Krueger's defense, given he is not present."

The potents shifted uncomfortably, several murmuring in surprise. Morvahna made a louder noise of disbelief and anger, although she schooled her expression when she felt the scrutiny of the others.

Dahlekov gaped at Lortus. "You are one of the parties wronged! He openly defied your orders!"

"Regardless," Lortus insisted, "I will speak for him. He has shown defiance, but that does not equate to being a traitor by our laws. We seek to foster initiative and independence in our subordinates so they may perform their functions. We cannot execute a druid of Krueger's accomplishments on such grounds. It is in keeping with our traditions"—here he clearly addressed Mohsar, Krueger's former master— "that he test the limits of our resolve."

Dahlekov gritted his teeth. "Confrontation is what Krueger seeks. An internal battle would weaken our order. We stand amid a war with the Legion of Everblight, an effort Krueger subverts at every opportunity." Morvahna nodded sharply at this, and several other potents made noises of agreement.

Mohsar said, "Lortus, you have spent decades following Blighterghast. I am surprised at your position. Krueger met with the dragon against your prohibition."

Lortus shook his head. "Krueger and I were in negotiations on the topic when Blighterghast's emissary invited the Stormwrath to an audience. The subsequent events would have transpired regardless of Krueger's actions." Dahlekov protested, but Lortus was unfazed. "So far as we are aware, the only information Krueger brought to Blighterghast was news of Everblight's attack on the Castle of the Keys. Eventually the dragons would have learned about Pyromalfic. Krueger's actions were rash, but I see no evidence of treachery. He has employed his army against Cryx, the trollkin kriels, and other enemies. Krueger is being true to his nature. He is a weapon we wield against our foes."

Krueger quickly rallied his remaining forces and charged down the slope to shatter the small group of reinforcements making their way up toward him. Woldwardens and woldwatchers made quick work of knights errant, and Krueger felt the rush of battle lust as he let Wurmtongue taste flesh before he sent sizzling bolts of lightning into whatever enemies he could reach. Despite this success, Krueger knew their actions atop the hill would soon enough attract additional attention. The massive army gathered below would make quick work of his vanguard if roused to turn on them in force.

For the moment, most of the enemy below faced the approaching army to the west. They were preparing lines of Deliverer rockets, supported by numerous Sunburst ballistae and several fully loaded Redeemer warjacks, each capable of delivering similar explosive barrages. Behind these were several thousand implacable Flameguard. Krueger's advancing forces were similarly numerous but came forward in a chaotic sprawl. So long as the Menites faced that threat, Krueger might pass behind them. It would be risky.

THE WOLDWARDENS PLUNGED INTO THE FRAY WITH GREAT STONY FISTS, TOWERING OVER THE ARMORED MENITES.

In moments the wayfarers and keepers Krueger had earlier dispatched returned with shifting stones, which rose up from the sands. The Stormlord put them to work preparing a teleport chain. Black-robed junior druids joined them, ready to lend their aid.

Knowing the woldwardens to be key to his success, Krueger sent them first. The keeper controlling the shifting stones invoked the runes and activated a triangle of power. The nearest woldwarden walked between the outer stones and vanished only to reappear close to the main refinery, where another set of stones launched it closer yet to the northern drill outfit. Krueger knew the woldwarden would not go unnoticed. The stones readied for the second woldwarden, who was sent ahead the same way.

Meanwhile Krueger hastened toward the main facility and the northern drilling platform beyond it. Graupel loped next to him, with the swift floating woldwyrds keeping pace. The shifting stones followed in their unique way, sinking into the ground before rising again nearer to the group, but they were soon left behind, as were the woldwatchers. The Protectorate army was still occupied to the west. Sunburst ballistae fired explosive-tipped spears in high arcs over the sands into the army of advancing Wolves and reeves.

A rear Flameguard officer spotted the peculiar group behind them and raised the alarm. Dozens of soldiers split off from the rear of the line to intercept. Krueger looked to Morraig and nodded that the wolf lord and his men should deal with them.

Similar to what he had done atop the hill, Krueger urged his woldwardens and woldwatchers to create an eruption of thorny life and knotted vegetation to screen their advance. Despite this, he spotted new enemies approaching from the drilling facility. These included not only additional rows of burnished Flameguard with spears at the ready but also

GREAT BALLS OF SPARKING WHITE-GREEN ENERGY EXPLODED ACROSS THE MENITE STRUCTURE.

Vanquisher and Castigator heavy warjacks and a pair each of Repenter and Redeemer light warjacks. At their center marched a striking woman in golden and white warcaster armor with elaborate smokestacks rising behind her back. A metal mask within a ceremonial priestess helmet obscured her face, and she bore a halberd-like weapon with a head that glowed with banked embers. Krueger recognized Feora, Priestess and Protector of the Flame, head of the Temple Flameguard.

A roar of fire from behind distracted Krueger. The Wolves and Reeves had taken shelter within the artificially erected barrier of thorns and trees, but a sudden inferno enveloped them. A row of Flameguard cleansers had disgorged their weapons to set the entire freshly conjured forest ablaze with gouts of Menoth's Fury. As the screams of Morraig's men rose above the sound of the flames, the Redeemer 'jacks fired a massive volley of rockets that spiraled toward Krueger. He summoned his whirlwind barely in time to provide a modicum of protection as explosions erupted around him.

At the tribunal, Dahlekov interrogated the other potents. They described how the force Krueger assembled had largely been stolen from other druids in the organization. There were very few regions that had not suffered some degree of defection to the so-called Stormlord. Morvahna spoke at length about the ways Krueger had undermined her efforts to confront the Legion of Everblight.

Mohsar finally cut her off. "We have the pertinent testimony. Let us call the vote and be done. Omnipotents, who among you deems Krueger guilty of the accusations?" Dahlekov

raised his hand immediately. After a moment, Mohsar raised his. There was an expectant pause, but Lortus shook his head.

Mohsar huffed in annoyance. "Per ancient laws, the penalty of death for a potent requires a sublime majority. Ideally this is met by a unanimous agreement of the omnipotents, which we lack. In the event of a single dissenting omnipotent, the consensus of the gathered potents can overturn the dissenter." He nodded to the potents. "Confer quickly."

Morvahna spoke first. "We know Krueger to be guilty. Should we arrive at this unanimously, I promise to do everything in my power to restore those resources and lands taken from each of you."

Bradigus Thorle scowled at her and groused in his deep voice, "Must we bargain like fishmongers?"

Morvahna was unperturbed. "Negotiations are allowed by the rules of conciliation. I do not ask you to vote against your conscience. But should you fear reprisal, I offer my support."

Donavus the Wornrock, eldest of the attending potents, spoke softly, "What if it were you on trial, Morvahna? Executing potents sets a dangerous precedent."

"I would expect to pay for my crimes. The evidence here is irrefutable. We must stand united—not only for those here, but also for those who are not." She closed her eyes and bowed her head briefly, then looked at them each in turn. After a moment she turned back to the omnipotents. "We are ready." She paused a moment and then said, "I find Krueger the Stormwrath guilty on both charges."

Mohsar cleared his throat. "And each of you?" Each potent voiced agreement, albeit several more hesitantly than others. Bradigus Thorle took the longest to affirm.

Mohsar nodded. "A sublime majority is achieved. Krueger the Stormwrath is judged guilty of fomenting insurrection and turning traitor. The sentence is death, to be carried out immediately." For the first time, Mohsar's voice sounded tired. "I will handle this personally; I know his capabilities best."

"That may not be necessary," Dahlekov said. "I set an agent in place against this likelihood."

Feora, Protector of the Flame, shouted, "Devourer filth! You interfere with the works of Menoth—this is something I will not allow!"

Krueger replied through his woldwardens. Compelled by his will they gathered energy, setting their runes aglow with bright green light before sending lightning streaking away to explode amid the advancing Flameguard. Krueger had maneuvered the wolds to stand ready to intercept the heavy armored warjacks. The Vanquisher retaliated with its flame belcher cannon, and a cannonball filled with Menoth's Fury exploded into the stone chest of one woldwarden. Orange fire raged along its ropes and wooden framework. The Castigator's fists erupted in flames as it ran heavily across the sand toward the other woldwarden.

Feora pointed her halberd, and bright orange runes outlined her hand while fire struck amid the nearest group of armored blackclads ahead of Krueger. Two ignited with white-hot fire that quickly reduced them to ash and melted slag. The other group heeded the shouted order of their warden and invoked disruptive magic to prevent further spells. Several of the druids mystically pulled rocks from the earth to hurl at Feora. She nimbly avoided most; her armor and power field absorbed the rest. A Repenter advanced to bathe several of the druids in flame.

Krueger let his pureblood release another great flesh-rending howl to tear through the advancing Flameguard, also impacting the nearest Redeemer and Repenter. His woldwyrds and woldwatchers added their blasts, although the armor on the 'jacks limited their effectiveness. The Castigator tromped through the hastily erected foliage surrounding the woldwarden and lifted its fiery fists to rain down blazing strikes one after the other, shattering fragments of stone from the construct's chest and lighting it afire. The woldwarden returned heavy blows like a pugilist. Its fist-runes lit with natural power, and then a surge of kinetic energy sent the eight-ton warjack flying back. The 'jack soon rose to its feet and shook its head as it readied to fight despite one arm hanging limp.

The fires and choking smoke rose around them. Krueger could not see what transpired between the larger armies preparing to clash to the west. Explosions from Repenter rockets continued to rain down, even as he sent one of his woldwatchers to engage one of those machines. A near blast sent shrapnel into his side, and he was forced to send the injury to a woldwyrd, cracking its stone façade. Despite the fire closing around him, he felt stubborn resolve. He knew he should be worried for his survival. It was not his promise to Wurmwood that drove him but determination to complete the task to which he had set his will.

Shifting stones rose around him at the behest of one of his keepers. Krueger gathered power from his bonded warbeasts and activated the stones. He flickered and vanished, reappearing past Feora to the north. He raised Wurmtongue and pointed it toward the drilling facility now in reach. He set loose multiple blasts of white lightning as he rose again into the air with glowing eyes. Great balls of sparking white-green energy exploded across the Menite

structure to shatter metal, wood, and stone. Again he felt the satisfaction of hearing machinery grind to pieces. Thick, unrefined oil spilled from the pipes across the desert sands.

Krueger turned to Feora. With the voice of thunder he cried, "All your efforts are undone!"

Before he could flee to rejoin his army, something abrasive seized his feet from below. He looked down to see the reaching limbs of a newly sprouted tree grasping him. Vines and leaves wrapped his waist and held him fast. Krueger felt his rage surge and glanced over his shoulder to where he sensed an invocation of natural power. On a ridge past the collapsing drilling refinery was a familiar blackclad form. "Wayfarer Tal," Krueger gasped. "You dare interfere?!"

The feeble attack should have been little more than an irritation, but the distraction sufficed to hold him in place long enough for the Protector of the Flame to close on him. Krueger turned to see she was lowering the head of her halberd at him. A gout of fire poured forth and turned the air around him into an inferno, catching his robes ablaze. The fire consumed the knotted roots that held him, but not quickly enough for him to escape the Repenter rockets fired upon him. He felt the impacts of the blasts even as fire bathed his limbs and crackled along his flesh with searing heat.

It took all his will and concentration to send his injuries away from himself, shattering the arm of one of his woldwardens and then tearing open a scorched wound on Graupel the pureblood, who struggled with the Vanquisher. Krueger fell from the air heavily. He felt the white-hot fire continue to burn despite all his effort to extinguish it. Somehow Feora's faith-fueled righteousness held his efforts at bay. In a moment of painful clarity he saw that she fed upon fire the way his order drank from the essence of Orboros.

Feora raised her hands to invoke a prayer so powerful it was beyond words. Golden light radiated around her as the swirling flames leapt to her will. She seemed lost in a passionate communion with the fire as her back arched and she rose from the ground. A conflagration burst across the landscape, igniting the freestanding pools of Menoth's Fury and setting afire Krueger's allies in a wide radius, along with every warbeast under his control. They blazed with supernal power he knew would not extinguish until even the stone had melted away. With sudden, dreadful clarity, Krueger saw the flames would reach the drilling pipes. The fire would follow the drill line to the unrefined Menoth's Fury below: the disaster Wurmwood had foreseen was about to transpire.

The fires on his warbeasts continued to rage, but Krueger retained his firm grasp and forced them nearer. He desperately siphoned their power to keep himself alive.

body. The woldwardens and woldwatchers disengaged. Ignoring their crumbling condition, he set them into a formation over the locus. The shifting stones arranged themselves as well and did what they could to keep the wolds from bursting apart, using restorative energies to knit stone and wood. It was an inexact replication of the stone sites dedicated to Orboros, a ring created to resonate with the power far below the sands. Each wold and the shifting stones sank into the earth as Krueger activated the attunement rite, seeking to connect the locus below with the full shining moon of Calder above. He sent his mind drilling downward. The strain of this effort was almost too great for his body to bear. He felt the desert sands leaching away his very vitality and desiccating his flesh. His eyes sank into his skull and his skin shriveled, but still he reached.

His head swam dangerously, but suddenly there was a connection. He did not need to open his eyes to know Wurmwood had arrived. The great tree appeared at the center of his improvised

One by one his woldwyrds shattered as he sent injuries to them. Walking slowly toward him, Feora seemed content to watch him burn.

Krueger was livid. He was the Stormlord! He could feel Orboros flowing through the desert; beneath the soil was an ocean of power, if only he could reach it. But here, outside the bounds of his territories and in a foreign element, tapping into that fulcrum would be almost impossible, and even the attempt could have disastrous consequences.

He ignored the fire consuming his skin and turning his armor into scalding brands. He gathered the winds and sent them forth as a hurricane. Green runes of power surrounded his

ring and sent roots downward. Cassius invoked his power in waves of natural destruction to obliterate Flameguard and batter warjacks. Feora summoned her 'jacks and gave a battle cry, intending to charge and deal with this newly arrived enemy. Meanwhile, souls of those who died were siphoned into the leafless branches of Wurmwood, while its roots eagerly drank the blood of those who fell. Everywhere men fell to spear or blade, it feasted upon their essence. Krueger felt those roots create a bridge to the ley line fulcrum.

Sudden strength roared up through the stone ring to fill him. A tide of natural power such as he had never experienced washed through his body and flung him high into the air. He laughed with it, maddened by the feel of it. The entire desert opened to him, and he invoked the storm.

The empty night sky buckled, and the stars and moons disappeared behind a dark blanket of heavy, pregnant clouds that emerged from nowhere. Lightning erupted over the landscape with rumbles of ear-shattering thunder, striking down to turn sand to glass. With a single outpouring of wind and pressure the air was filled with heavy rain: no simple downpour but a flood of water, as if drawn from the distant ocean through some unnatural intermediary. The salty water tasted like blood as it flowed down to wash the sands from beneath Feora, sending her and her soldiers tumbling. As she was swept away the fires lost their unnatural potency and were quenched. Choking and drowning within the torrent of wind and water, friend and foe alike scrambled for anchorage. He shouted, "Where is your god now?"

Krueger cackled with mad delight as lightning poured from him in streaks by the dozen. He shattered the central refinery structure, then sent bolts chasing into Menite soldiers and the warjacks beneath. Spotting Wayfarer Tal rooted awestruck by the display, Krueger reached with a tendril of air to seize hold of the treacherous druid. With a single yank Krueger pulled Tal screaming high into the air and then dropped him to plunge to his death.

The conduit of energy between him and Wurmwood combined with the torrential downpour destabilized the very earth. Deep below the sands the repository of oil the Menites had sought was shifted, its fluids broken free to flow down freshly opened channels deeper into the earth. In the great hollow place where the oil had been, the ground sank. Below Krueger a sinkhole devoured a region of sands wider than the entire chain of Menite structures.

Krueger felt the energy leave him as his access to the torrent of power shut off so abruptly it made his head ring. Wurmwood was no longer there, nor was Cassius, and he saw no sign of the damaged wolds he had used to create his sacred ring. Krueger flew down amid the heavy rain to return to his army, savoring the last few lightning strikes that lit the sky. His robes and armor were reduced to loosely connected tatters and his skin scarred from burns, but those gathered bowed in awestruck humility. He saw Wolf Lord Morraig had escaped the tumult and said to him, "We must depart before the Menites gather their wits."

"What of Wurmwood?" Morraig asked.

Krueger looked to the devastation. "The Tree of Fate has answered. When we have need, it will come."

The potents were preparing to disperse when there was a ripple of power. Into the conclave's midst had arrived the unmistakable tree Wurmwood, rooted as if it had always been there between the two great towering cairns. Cassius was alongside the tree, wrapped in roots, his expression inscrutable.

The Oathkeeper spoke. "Hold! This tribunal is not concluded."

Lortus was the first to find his tongue. "Cassius, your presence honors us, as does that of the special plenipotentiary, Wurmwood. It has been long since we have been graced with the wisdom offered by the Tree of Fate and its chosen conduit."

"My business here will be brief. I know what brings you together. I will speak on this matter. I affirm Krueger the Stormlord is no traitor to the Circle Orboros."

This prompted a stir, particularly from Morvahna, who sputtered with rage. "The verdict is decided! Sentence was passed!" Bradigus Thorle pulled her back before she could approach Cassius.

Mohsar turned toward her sharply. "Silence! Do not force me to revoke your rank." The blood left Morvahna's face, and her stare filled with cold rage as several of the other potents gave her pitying looks.

Lortus spoke more gently. "The Tree of Fate has the right to offer opinion when the omnipotents are not in unanimous accord. The vote cast by Cassius for Wurmwood has greater weight than that of the collective potents, by ancient law."

Mohsar nodded grimly and confirmed, "The sublime majority is broken. The sentence of death is rescinded." Dahlekov's face was red. Morvahna stood pale with shock among the muttering potents.

The hubbub died away as Cassius raised his blade. His voice was deeper and his words spoken slower, as if unfiltered through human sensibilities. "Know this! The Stormlord is my chosen oracle of the apocalypse. The coming of the dragons will invoke a tide of blood and cause fire and ash to rain down to destroy anything they touch. The wounds of Orboros will be scoured by slaughter so that healing may begin. We enter a time of upheaval. The civilizations of man tremble upon the precipice of ruin."

The gathered potents stared, unable to move. In another moment, Wurmwood and Cassius vanished, as if they had never been present.

The Circle Orboros is the most ancient human organization extant in western Immoren, the product of thousands of years of coordinated efforts to master the powers of nature. Few outside its inner cabal suspect it is anything but a disorganized group of enigmatic if individually potent blackclad druids and their personal armies. Operating in scattered groups, the blackclads have created a network of sacred sites to channel natural power. By this network the druids can communicate and travel across vast distances and have become versed in overseeing and protecting myriad fastnesses of the wilds. When roused to war, the Circle Orboros is unsurpassed at exploiting terrain to their advantage, in striking swiftly and unexpectedly across great distances, and in invoking destructive elemental power. Storm thunders by their will, stones rise from the earth with a gesture, and terrifying beasts rage at their command.

Those loyal to the blackclads make their homes in the wilds of every nation and in every sizable forest, mountain range, swamp, and desert. Families live in these remote corners who are bound to the druids by ancient ties and who stand ready to lend their strength. Barbaric peoples have willingly entered into alliance with the blackclads, and the druids manipulate other warlike species to fight on their behalf. When the Circle gathers for war, it does so as it has for millennia: at the head of a howling horde that would smash the cities of man and cast humanity into an everlasting dark age.

CUSTODIANS OF THE APOCALYPSE

Outsiders believe blackclads are priests of the Devourer Wurm, a primal force of destruction and the ancient foe of Menoth, the Creator of Man. In truth the druids do not worship the Devourer so much as placate it. Blackclads recognize the Wurm as the conscious aspect of the primal entity Orboros, and they work to ensure it remains distracted by its eternal war in Urcaen against Menoth. What exists on Caen, and what provides the druids' mystical power, is the unthinking body of Orboros. Their labors maintaining the ley line energies that are this body's circulatory system ensure it remains strong. These invisible arteries and veins can become choked by civilization: anything that disrupts the flow of rivers, the integrity of the mountains and hills, or the growth cycles of forests injures Orboros. When its body becomes too riddled with wounds left by the cities of civilizations, the Devourer Wurm will realize its weakening condition and return to the world to unleash unparalleled devastation and exterminate humanity.

The Circle Orboros believes this apocalypse inevitable. Civilization increasingly pushes back the natural world, and even incessant warfare between nations has not diminished mankind's populations. Facing this, the blackclads insist violence on any scale against civilization is justified. Even were all the great kingdoms shattered, it would not be enough to reverse this imbalance, which pushes the druids to ever-greater acts of destruction.

In this cause the Circle willingly allies with cultists and barbarians. Blackclads have a deserved reputation for callousness and an uncaring attitude toward slaughter, plague, and famine. Despite this reputation, their larger work is bent toward forestalling far greater destruction. They ultimately seek to preserve a place for humanity on Caen.

In meeting this ancient duty there is no stretch of wilderness in western Immoren outside their dominion. Their scattered territories and the placement of their towering circles of mystical stones seem random to outsiders but are carefully chosen based on the order's understanding of the way power flows through the body of Orboros. They continually work to identify, liberate, and tap into the energies that entangle the wild places of the world. Druids believe the movements of

TRANSPORT BY STONE

The uncanny ease with which blackclads and their allies can muster has long unnerved their enemies. Border patrols and sentries are useless against them; the Circle has many means to gather its forces, and their knowledge of wilderness terrain and secret byways is a considerable aid, as are the swiftness and endurance of their warriors. But the greatest asset to these movements is the network of ley line nodes and sacred sites protected by the order. Through complex and difficult mystical rites druids can tap into these energy flows to merge with the arteries of Orboros and emerge almost instantaneously elsewhere. Powerfully enchanted shifting stones serve as extensions of this network.

The highest-ranking druids know the rites to transport themselves to their sacred sites, but these mysteries are the specialty of wayfarers. Wayfarers possess such mastery they can send themselves much farther abroad than their peers can. For this reason wayfarers are tasked to carry vital messages between druids and often accompany the order's leaders.

Utilizing this network to move sizable numbers of soldiers is far more difficult and requires larger stones at major ley line intersection sites, where exponentially more power converges. This may also require astrological alignments and the simultaneous efforts of multiple druids and wayfarers. Therefore armies usually travel traditionally—over land—though wayfarers can more easily expedite smaller groups of reinforcements across vast distances.

TERRITORIAL DOMINIONS OF THE CIRCLE ORBOROS

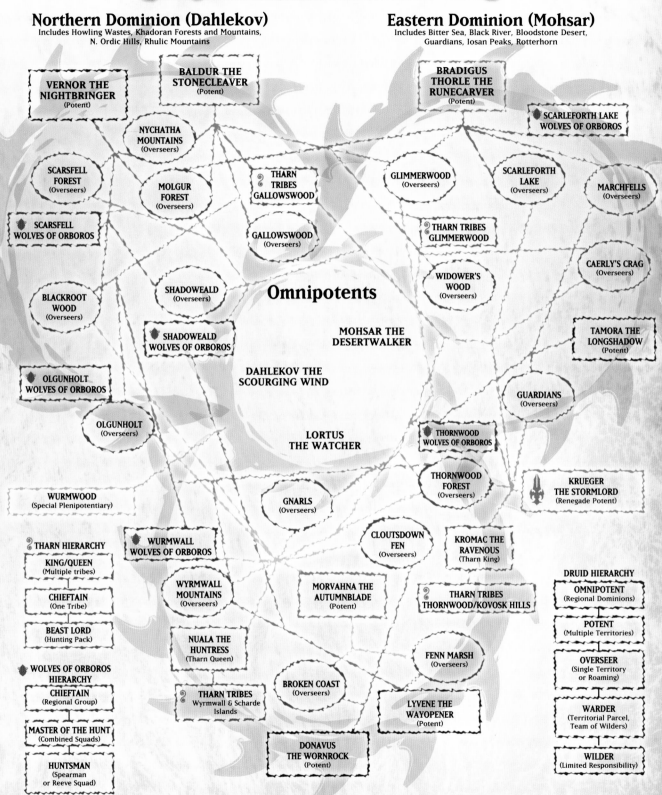

Northern Dominion (Dahlekov)
Includes Howling Wastes, Khadoran Forests and Mountains,
N. Ordic Hills, Rhulic Mountains

VERNOR THE NIGHTBRINGER
(Potent)

BALDUR THE STONECLEAVER
(Potent)

NYCHATHA MOUNTAINS
(Overseers)

SCARSFELL FOREST
(Overseers)

MOLGUR FOREST
(Overseers)

THARN TRIBES GALLOWSWOOD

SCARSFELL WOLVES OF ORBOROS

GALLOWSWOOD
(Overseers)

BLACKROOT WOOD
(Overseers)

SHADOWEALD
(Overseers)

SHADOWEALD WOLVES OF ORBOROS

OLGUNHOLT WOLVES OF ORBOROS

OLGUNHOLT
(Overseers)

Omnipotents

MOHSAR THE DESERTWALKER

DAHLEKOV THE SCOURGING WIND

LORTUS THE WATCHER

Eastern Dominion (Mohsar)
Includes Bitter Sea, Black River, Bloodstone Desert,
Guardians, Iosan Peaks, Rotterhorn

BRADIGUS THORLE THE RUNECARVER
(Potent)

SCARLEFORTH LAKE WOLVES OF ORBOROS

GLIMMERWOOD
(Overseers)

SCARLEFORTH LAKE
(Overseers)

MARCHFELLS
(Overseers)

THARN TRIBES GLIMMERWOOD

WIDOWER'S WOOD
(Overseers)

CAERLY'S CRAG
(Overseers)

TAMORA THE LONGSHADOW
(Potent)

GUARDIANS
(Overseers)

THORNWOOD WOLVES OF ORBOROS

THORNWOOD FOREST
(Overseers)

KRUEGER THE STORMLORD
(Renegade Potent)

WURMWOOD
(Special Plenipotentiary)

GNARLS
(Overseers)

CLOUTSDOWN FEN
(Overseers)

KROMAC THE RAVENOUS
(Tharn King)

WURMWALL WOLVES OF ORBOROS

WYRMWALL MOUNTAINS
(Overseers)

MORVAHNA THE AUTUMNBLADE
(Potent)

THARN TRIBES THORNWOOD/KOVOSK HILLS

NUALA THE HUNTRESS
(Tharn Queen)

FENN MARSH
(Overseers)

THARN TRIBES
Wyrmwall & Scharde Islands

BROKEN COAST
(Overseers)

LYVENE THE WAYOPENER
(Potent)

DONAVUS THE WORNROCK
(Potent)

THARN HIERARCHY

KING/QUEEN
(Multiple tribes)

CHIEFTAIN
(One Tribe)

BEAST LORD
(Hunting Pack)

WOLVES OF ORBOROS HIERARCHY

CHIEFTAIN
(Regional Group)

MASTER OF THE HUNT
(Combined Squads)

HUNTSMAN
(Spearman or Reeve Squad)

DRUID HIERARCHY

OMNIPOTENT
(Regional Dominions)

POTENT
(Multiple Territories)

OVERSEER
(Single Territory or Roaming)

WARDER
(Territorial Parcel, Team of Wilders)

WILDER
(Limited Responsibility)

Southern Dominion (Lortus)
Includes the Gnarls, Olgunholt, Thornwood, Broken Coast Islands, Wyrmwall Mountains

IMMEDIATE THREATS TO ORBOROS

The Circle Orboros is not alone in its awareness of the energies running beneath the soils of Caen. Both the Cult of Cyriss and the arcanists of Ios are aware of these wellsprings of power and make use of them to fuel their technological constructs. The Cult of Cyriss has had little impact on most of western Immoren, being small in scope and extremely secretive and preferring to hide its temples in remote locations. Yet for these very reasons the worshipers of the Maiden of Gears are frequently in competition with the Circle Orboros over important ley line nodes. The cult describes these energies differently and studies them under the guise of scientific methods, but the underlying principles are identical. When Cyrissists drain these energies, it disrupts the flow of the channels the same way a dam diverts the natural flow of a river. Cyrissists are adept at integrating their temples into cities and other urban areas, allowing them to tap nodes the Circle Orboros cannot reach. Arcanists of the elven Retribution of Scyrah have yet to compete actively with the Circle over their control of nodes in human lands, but their increased activity in recent years makes such confrontations inevitable.

Toruk, Everblight, and the other dragons represent something far worse. Dragon blight can annihilate the natural flows altogether. In addition to its malignant effects on living creatures, dragon blight taints and corrupts the land, seeping into the soil and rock to poison the very body of Orboros. The Circle has developed techniques to correct and mitigate this, but such solutions are unreliable. The Scharde Islands, for example, were once fertile with natural energies, but now those innermost islands of Cryx are useless for druidic rites due to the pervasive blight of Lord Toruk. Similarly, the recently arisen Legion of Everblight is considered an urgent threat by high-ranking druids due to the alarming proliferation of dragonspawn as well as evidence of blighted energies wielded as weapons of war.

the stars and planets are mystically tied to the ebb and flow of Orboros' lifeblood; by combining knowledge of ley lines with celestial conjunctions, they enact extraordinarily potent rites.

The Circle armies exist in part to protect these mystical nodes and vital territories, and the martial might of the order is concentrated in these places. Some of the richest fonts for the natural power of Orboros are situated in regions of interest to civilized kingdoms, such as near major rivers and mountain passes. This includes places like the mouth of the Black River, where Caspia and Sul represent one of the oldest and most lasting injuries inflicted by civilization on the body of Orboros.

To master this energy flow, druids must become obsessed with personal power. Blackclads are few in number, and so it is the responsibility of each to become formidable. They must put survival first, even if it means sacrificing others. The order is simultaneously hierarchical and populated by fiercely independent individuals, each with a personal interpretation of the order's goals. As each druid becomes a master of the elements, he accumulates allies, guardians, and beasts of war. These can be combined to create large fighting forces.

While the inevitable apocalypse of the Devourer Wurm's return looms, the Circle must attend to more immediate threats. Blackclads strive daily to defend sacred sites from rivals and to deal with other perils to Orboros, such as the malignancy of dragon blight. For most druids, the worsening balance between Orboros and civilization is a distant abstraction that has little to do with day-to-day struggles.

HIERARCHY OF THE BLACKCLADS

Though the Circle employs a variety of allies and minions, it is the druids who rule the faction and make the key decisions. There are echelons of power, authority, and knowledge within their own ranks, as Circle leaders are cautious with the order's lore. Members must earn advancement before occupying leadership positions or being entrusted with the oversight of large territories. The Circle safeguards layers upon layers of secrets, and only the topmost leaders understand the organization's inner workings. This system has served for thousands of years to reward the skilled and ambitious while limiting those who fail to meet the Circle's unforgiving standards.

Each blackclad is born with the potential for almost endless power. This is called the *wilding*, and it is believed to be an innate connection to Orboros through the arbitrary selection of the Devourer Wurm. Because this ability cannot be taught, it is vitally important for the Circle to find such individuals as early as possible and provide them with the training to control their powers. Should the parents of a child undergoing the wilding be intractable, blackclads have no compunctions about stealing him. Some people assume such children are slated as sacrifices in profane rites, which contributes to the Circle's sinister reputation.

Over the centuries the Circle has refined its mystical methods to find children with this ability regardless of where they are born. These efforts are aided by the fact that the Circle has records of bloodlines known to manifest the wilding. Many of these families are bound to the Wolves of Orboros who serve as the order's soldiers. Unlike outsiders, these families are familiar with the signs of the wilding and willingly surrender children displaying such signs to the druids.

the Ten Ills. This prompted a legacy of infertility among the Tharn and pushed them into severe decline, their numbers dwindling so dramatically some thought them a vanished people. Approximately thirty years ago this curse was broken by Morvahna the Autumnblade, who not only restored Tharn fertility but amplified it tremendously, prompting a surge in births including twins and triplets. The Tharn have rapidly regained their former numbers and stature and have demonstrated their appreciation for this miraculous intervention by committing utterly and completely to the wars of the blackclads.

Of varied composition, Tharn war bands are fierce but only loosely organized. Males and females contribute equally to battle. Ravagers are the heavy frontline terror warriors. These males channel the power of the Devourer to transform into larger, more muscular, and hardier forms; each axe-wielding ravager is capable of horrendous slaughter, particularly when backed by their shamans. Bloodtrackers, the most numerous of the female Tharn warriors, provide an agile counterpoint to the ravagers. These hunters are experts in hurling javelins and will strike from the flanks and the rear against their chosen prey, channeling the Devourer to gain supernatural speed and to augment their predatory senses. Similar to the bloodtrackers are the wolf riders, who ride their savage mounts to gain even greater mobility, momentum,

and killing power. Other Tharn such as the ravager shamans and the female bloodweavers draw on Tharn blood magic to lend their support, slaughtering their enemies to enact gruesomely effective bloodletting rituals.

Tharn society is chaotic and primal, with the strong ruling the weak. Life is a swift and unforgiving cycle of battles and revelry. They are a fierce and passionate people but also loyal to those who have earned their respect. Bands of Tharn warriors are led by beast lords, while tribes called *tuaths* are led by chieftains. Given the violence of their society, longevity requires peerless skill; eager to seize their own glory, the young watch their elders for any sign of weakness.

While most Tharn tuaths are isolated, periodically notable chieftains rise to special stature as kings and queens. Theoretically any chief can call himself a king, but without widespread recognition it is a hollow boast that will provoke violent challenges. Recognized kings and queens of the Tharn—such as Kromac the Ravenous and Nuala the Huntress—command the loyalty of dozens of village-sized tribes across a wide region and are feared even outside their customary territories.

Communications and coordination between druids and Tharn is fluid, though Tharn will generally heed any blackclad who comes to them. In cases of competing claims

THE FALL AND RETURN OF THE THARN

During the war between Khador's Queen Cherize and Cygnar's King Malagant less than a hundred years after the Corvis Treaties, the Tharn joined the conflict on the side of the Khadorans. Cygnaran historical records paint the Tharn in a black light during this conflict and suggest they were corrupted by Thamarites, who were allegedly behind Queen Cherize's rise to power. What is not known to historians is that the Circle Orboros encouraged Tharn involvement in this fight, hoping to destabilize both kingdoms. These struggles had the intended effect, weakening both monarchies while helping permanently undermine the power of the Menite faith within Cygnar, which was experiencing a shift in its state religion.

The omnipotents of the Circle Orboros had a vested interest in seeing Cygnar adopt the Morrowan faith and therefore further weaken the Menite temples. This was part of a larger plan to weaken Menoth in Urcaen to compensate for the damage done by the spread of civilization to Orboros. However, the omnipotents did not anticipate the Morrowan backlash that would be directed at the Tharn, who were accused of being abominations and creatures of darkness.

The greatest Morrowan priests invoked holy retribution on the surviving tribes. The so-called "Curse of the Ten Ills" proved to be a tremendously powerful and debilitating affliction that defeated all subsequent attempts by both Tharn shamans and druids of the Circle to correct it.

The curse nearly proved the end of these tribes, weakened as they were by warfare casualties. For nearly three centuries the Tharn suffered under this affliction, finding birth rates insufficient to replenish their numbers. It was not until Morvahna the Autumnblade bent her considerable power and skill to this dilemma that hope was restored. Morvahna, who had already proven to be a master of living vitality, conducted an empowered rite under the auspices of a rare conjunction of Caen's moons with a planet called the Eye of the Wurm. At the peak of this ceremony and with the Tharn offering the sacrifices of numerous captured enemies, the affliction was unraveled. Morvahna's rivals believe the curse may have simply been weakening from the passage of so many generations, but the Tharn believe Morvahna to be the instrument of their salvation.

weapons. For more than a thousand years the Circle's beast masters have slowly evolved the process of creating them. They once used certain alchemical mixtures to help catalyze this transformation but eventually eliminated these rudimentary aids in favor of rituals conducted at powerful ley line nodes during conjunctions of Caen's three moons. Once battle is over, an exhausted feral warpwolf returns to human guise, but its mind is forever altered: just like the Tharn, warpwolves have diverged from their human origins. Even in their human form, first-generation warpwolves are deranged and suffer from predatory urges, extremely violent impulses, and an inability to control their tempers.

Once transformed, warpwolves can breed and produce young that carry their transformative power but that suffer from a slightly reduced form of their mental instability. After several generations, certain of these progeny are "pureblood" and no longer revert to human form. Besides being calmer and more accepting of their nature than feral warpwolves, purebloods possess striking intelligence, but their minds are not human. Even to Circle beast masters, they are an enigmatic and unpredictable breed.

Druids continue to refine their beast creation process, seeking a perfect balance between human intelligence and predatory rage. One of the great successes of these efforts is the warpborn skinwalkers, warriors taken from among zealous Wolves of Orboros to become something greater. While not as robust or deadly as feral warpwolves, skinwalkers retain their intelligence. The Circle may eventually find other ways to unleash the bestial reserves of primal power buried in the hearts and souls of mankind.

between druids, Tharn fall back on personal relationships and oaths. The blackclads have never had to resort to the subtler manipulations or deceptions they frequently have employed to enlist trollkin kriels or wary groups of gatormen, farrow, bog trogs, or other wilderness species. Tharn are entirely willing to revel in unleashing their rage by joining battle, no matter the reason.

MAN OR BEAST?

The line between man and beast becomes blurred in the Circle. Blackclads have developed a wide assortment of powerful weapons, including those built by their own hands in stone and wood as well as living beasts tamed or subdued from the deep wilds. Yet some of their greatest successes relate to unlocking the beast within the minds and bodies of what were once ordinary human beings.

Warpwolves owe their origins to such techniques, inspired in part from the manner in which Tharn channel the Devourer Wurm. The hideously strong, swift, and adaptable warpwolves have become one of the Circle's greatest

CIRCLE THEME FORCES

BALDUR THE STONECLEAVER
ROCK OF ORBOROS

WARBEASTS
Circle non-character construct warbeasts, Megalith

UNITS
Druids of Orboros, Druid Stoneward & Woldstalkers, Sentry Stone & Mannikins, Shifting Stones

SOLOS
Blackclad Wayfarer, Druid Wilder

TIER 1
Requirements: The army can include only the models listed above.

Benefit: Sentry Stone & Mannikin units can be placed up to 20" from the back edge of Baldur's deployment zone.

TIER 2
Requirements: The army includes one or more Shifting Stone units and one or more Sentry Stone & Mannikin units.

Benefit: Up to one warbeast in Baldur's battlegroup gains Advance Deployment ⬤ for each Shifting Stone or Sentry Stone & Mannikin unit in the army.

TIER 3
Requirements: The army includes two Druid Stoneward & Woldstalker units.

Benefit: Druid Stoneward & Woldstalker units gain Advance Move. (Before the start of the game but after both players have deployed, a model with Advance Move can make a full advance.)

TIER 4
Requirements: The army includes Megalith.

Benefit: Reduce the point cost of heavy warbeasts by 1.

CASSIUS THE OATHKEEPER
WIDOWER'S WOOD

WARBEASTS
Circle construct warbeasts, Circle heavy warbeasts

UNITS
Druids of Orboros, Reeves of Orboros, Sentry Stone & Mannikins, Shifting Stones, Warpborn Skinwalkers

SOLOS
Feralgeist, Reeve Hunters, War Wolves, Lord of the Feast

TIER 1
Requirements: The army can include only the models listed above.

Benefit: Warpborn Skinwalker units become FA U. Additionally, increase the FA of War Wolves by +1 for each unit in the army.

TIER 2
Requirements: The army includes two or more Warpborn Skinwalker units.

Benefit: Your deployment zone is extended 2" forward.

TIER 3
Requirements: The army includes the Lord of the Feast.

Benefit: Wurmwood begins the game with three soul tokens.

TIER 4
Requirements: Cassius' army includes one or more Warpwolf Stalkers.

Benefit: Models/units in this army gain Stealth ⬤ during the first round of the game.

KAYA THE WILDBORNE
THE WILD HUNT

WARBEASTS
Living Circle non-character warbeasts

UNITS
Reeves of Orboros, Tharn Bloodtrackers, Tharn Wolf Riders, Wolves of Orboros

SOLOS
Druid Wilder, Reeve Hunter, War Wolf, Wolf Lord Morraig

TIER 1

Requirements: The army can include only the models listed above.

Benefit: Reduce the point cost of Reeves of Orboros units by 1. Additionally, increase the FA of War Wolf solos by +1 for every Reeves of Orboros unit in the army.

TIER 2

Requirements: The army includes Wolf Lord Morraig.

Benefit: One Wolves of Orboros unit gains Advance Move. (Before the start of the game but after both players have deployed, a model with Advance Move can make a full advance.)

TIER 3

Requirements: Your army includes one or more Reeves of Orboros unit.

Benefit: For each Reeves of Orboros unit in the army, place one 4″ AOE forest template anywhere completely within 20″ of the back edge of Kaya's deployment zone after terrain has been placed but before either player deploys his army. Forest templates cannot be placed within 3″ of another terrain feature, including other forest templates.

TIER 4

Requirements: Kaya's battlegroup includes two or more heavy warbeasts.

Benefit: Your deployment zone is extended 2″ forward.

KAYA THE MOONHUNTER
CALL OF THE WILD

WARBEASTS
Living Circle non-character warbeasts

UNITS
Druids of Orboros, Shifting Stones, Warpborn Skinwalkers

SOLOS
Druid Wilder, War Wolf

TIER 1

Requirements: The army can include only the models listed above.

Benefit: Heavy warbeasts in Kaya's battlegroup gain Advance Deployment ⏩.

TIER 2

Requirements: The army includes one or more Warpborn Skinwalker units.

Benefit: Warpborn Skinwalkers gain Advance Move. (Before the start of the game but after both players have deployed, a model with Advance Move can make a full advance.)

TIER 3

Requirements: The army includes one or more Druids of Orboros units.

Benefit: You gain +1 on your starting game roll.

TIER 4

Requirements: Kaya's battlegroup includes two or more heavy warbeasts.

Benefit: Reduce the point cost of heavy warbeasts by 1.

KRUEGER THE STORMWRATH
STORM FRONT

WARBEASTS
Circle non-character warbeasts

UNITS
Druids of Orboros, Shifting Stones, Wolves of Orboros

SOLOS
Blackclad Wayfarer, Druid Wilder, Wolf Lord Morraig

TIER 1
Requirements: The army can include only the models listed above.

Benefit: Druids of Orboros units and unit attachments become FA U. Additionally, increase the FA of Blackclad Wayfarer solos by +1 for each Druid of Orboros unit in the army.

TIER 2
Requirements: The army includes Wolf Lord Morraig.

Benefit: You gain +1 on your starting game roll.

TIER 3
Requirements: The army includes two or more Druids of Orboros units.

Benefit: Reduce the point cost of Druids of Orboros units by 1.

TIER 4
Requirements: Krueger's battlegroup includes two or more heavy warbeasts.

Benefit: Warbeasts in Krueger's battlegroup gain +2 SPD during your first turn of the game.

KRUEGER THE STORMLORD
THE DEVOURER'S HOST

WARBEASTS
Living Circle non-character warbeasts

UNITS
Tharn Ravagers, Warpborn Skinwalkers

SOLOS
Tharn Ravager solos, Lord of the Feast

TIER 1
Requirements: The army can include only the models listed above.

Benefit: Tharn Ravager units become FA U.

TIER 2
Requirements: The army includes the Lord of the Feast.

Benefit: Tharn Ravager units and the Lord of the Feast each begin the game with one corpse token.

TIER 3
Requirements: The army includes two or more Tharn Ravager units.

Benefit: Tharn Ravager models/units gain +2 SPD during your first turn of the game.

TIER 4
Requirements: Krueger's battlegroup includes two or more Warpwolves.

Benefit: Warpwolves in Krueger's battlegroup gain Advance Move. (Before the start of the game but after both players have deployed, a model with Advance Move can make a full advance.)

KROMAC THE RAVENOUS
HEART EATERS

WARBEASTS	UNITS	SOLOS
Circle non-character living warbeasts	Tharn units	Tharn solos, Lord of the Feast

TIER 1

Requirements: The army can include only the models listed above.

Benefit: Tharn Ravager units and weapon attachments become FA U. Additionally, increase the FA of Tharn Ravager White Mane solos by +1 for each unit in the army.

TIER 2

Requirements: The army includes two or more Tharn Ravager units.

Benefit: Add a unit attachment to one Tharn Ravager unit free of cost. This unit attachment ignores FA restrictions.

TIER 3

Requirements: The army includes two or more Tharn Ravager White Mane solos.

Benefit: For every two solos in the army, one heavy warbeast in Kromac's battlegroup gains Advance Move. (Before the start of the game but after both players have deployed, a model with Advance Move can make a full advance.)

TIER 4

Requirements: The army includes Lord of the Feast.

Benefit: Models in Kromac's battlegroup gain Stealth ⓘ during the first round of the game.

MOHSAR THE DESERTWALKER
SANDSTORM

WARBEASTS	UNITS	SOLOS
Circle non-character warbeasts	Druid Stoneward & Woldstalkers, Reeves of Orboros, Sentry Stone & Mannikins, Shifting Stones, Druid units	Blackclad Wayfarer, Reeve Hunters, War Wolves, Lord of the Feast

TIER 1

Requirements: The army can include only the models listed above.

Benefit: Models in Mohsar's battlegroup gain Apparition during your first turn of the game. (During your Control Phase, place models with Apparition anywhere completely within 2″ of their current locations. If this affects a unit, only models in formation can be placed.)

TIER 2

Requirements: The army includes one or more Druid Stoneward & Woldstalker units.

Benefit: Druid Stoneward & Woldstalker units can be redeployed after both players have deployed but before the first player's first turn. The redeployed models must be placed on the table in a location they could have been deployed initially.

TIER 3

Requirements: The army includes two Druids of Orboros units.

Benefit: Add a unit attachment to one Druids of Orboros unit free of cost. This unit attachment ignores FA restrictions.

TIER 4

Requirements: The army includes two or more heavy warbeasts.

Benefit: For each heavy warbeast in Mohsar's battlegroup, place one 3″ AOE anywhere completely within 20″ of the back edge of Mohsar's deployment zone after terrain has been placed but before either player deploys his army. The AOEs are obstructions that block LOS and provide cover. They are structures with ARM 18 that leave play if they suffer 1 or more damage points.

MORVAHNA THE AUTUMNBLADE
HARVEST OF BLOOD

WARBEASTS
Circle non-character light warbeasts

UNITS
Druids of Orboros, Tharn Bloodtrackers, Tharn Bloodweavers, Tharn Wolf Riders, Shifting Stones

SOLOS
Blackclad Wayfarer, Druid Wilder, War Wolves

TIER 1
Requirements: The army can include only the models listed above.

Benefit: Tharn Bloodtracker and Tharn Bloodweaver units become FA 3.

TIER 2
Requirements: The army includes one or more Tharn Bloodtracker units.

Benefit: Add Nuala the Huntress to one Tharn Bloodtracker unit free of cost.

TIER 3
Requirements: The army includes two or more Tharn Bloodweaver units.

Benefit: Friendly models/units can begin the game affected by Morvahna's upkeep spells. These spells and their targets must be declared before either player sets up models. Morvahna does not pay focus to upkeep these spells during your first turn.

TIER 4
Requirements: The army includes one Tharn Wolf Rider unit.

Benefit: Your deployment zone is extended 2″ forward.

WARLOCKS OF THE CIRCLE

In the Circle Orboros the term "warlock" is rarely used, as this role is simply a normal extension of a druid's power. In fact, virtually all Circle warlocks are druids. Being a warlock is a minor distinction related to the more specific ability to bind and command the warbeasts that answer the call of the blackclads, including the mighty natural constructs called wolds. This refined ability requires a druid of experience and skill, and a warlock who has mastered it becomes a formidable battlefield leader. All the top-ranking leaders of the Circle Orboros possess this capability, and no one below the rank of overseer has ever managed it. Often the very mention of these enigmatic individuals' names is enough to evoke disquiet or outright fear among those who live in the wild places of western Immoren.

Like all druids, Circle warlocks do not choose to join and lead their brethren; instead, they are born with a mysterious power called the *wilding*, which is believed to be an innate connection to the Devourer Wurm. This connection, poorly understood by those outside the Circle, taps into the primal power of the natural world and is linked to the concepts of elemental chaos and predation as well as the energy and stones that form the blood and bones of Caen.

The wilding is a powerful and unpredictable force that must be harnessed, tamed, and shaped by years of training and study, so all young Circle druids undergo a lengthy period of mentoring with a veteran blackclad. Because of the early age at which the wilding manifests, this serves as the only upbringing druids will remember, which leaves them viewing the world differently than people raised in civilization.

During this mentoring a druid learns the nature of his or her power, how to control it, and the fundamental philosophies of Orboros. While mentors provide wilders with an essential foundation, the most important aspect of this training is teaching the young druid how to define his own path and refine his powers over time. Each druid will follow a different course to unlocking his full potential, which may include a unique specialization in one or more aspects of the natural power of Orboros. Whatever their ultimate expertise, all druids learn some modicum of control over the beasts and constructs that serve as weapons of war. Subordinate druids assist in the handling and movement of these vital assets, but such abilities are a pale shadow of the mastery warlocks possess.

Few blackclads advance in rank and power sufficiently to learn the binding rites and other beast-related skills they must have as warlocks. The warbeasts used by the Circle are not permanently bound to a specific warlock, but before battle each must be temporarily joined to the druid who will be controlling it in battle and using its inner rage to empower his or her combat prowess. Once bound, these beasts can be directed with but a thought by the controlling warlock, who can also push them beyond their physical

THE WILDING

The *wilding* resides within the souls of all who have been touched by Orboros, and for druids it represents the ability to command the powers of creation. It typically manifests very early, generally between the ages of five and ten. A child in the throes of the wilding displays markedly strange behavior such as sneaking out into the night to howl at the moon, responding to voices he hears upon the wind, or emulating the behavior of beasts. This is a result of the child trying to make sense of the world as he begins to perceive the power of nature all around him. Unless they have some connection to the Circle, often the family of such youngsters believe their child has gone mad or has become possessed by evil spirits. It is no wonder that many parents willingly give up such a child when a blackclad appears to claim him.

BALDUR THE STONECLEAVER

limits. Druids who become warlocks learn how to draw upon the inner essence of the beasts to manifest powerful mystical effects called *animi*. Perhaps the most important element of this bond is that it enables druids to shunt wounds intended for them to the bodies of their beasts instead. Particularly given their scarcity, warlocks must make use of every expediency to stay alive and continue to wage war for the Circle Orboros.

Circle warlocks are deeply political and savagely ambitious, engaging in far-reaching schemes against one another that can take decades to come to fruition. These rivalries rarely develop into outright confrontations; most warlocks prefer to work through minions to undermine rivals' activities. Like nature itself, the Circle Orboros rewards only the strongest, smartest, and most determined druid with power and position.

BALDUR THE STONECLEAVER
CIRCLE WARLOCK

Baldur is the Rock of Orboros. Let our enemies crash against his strength like the waters of the tide.

—Omnipotent Dahlekov

BALDUR

SPD	STR	MAT	RAT	DEF	ARM	CMD
5	7	7	4	14	16	8

TRITUS

	POW	P+S
	7	14

FURY	6
DAMAGE	17
FIELD ALLOWANCE	C
WARBEAST POINTS	+6
SMALL BASE	

FEAT: BROKEN EARTH

For Baldur earth and stone are living things—the skin and bones of Orboros. Boulders spring from the ground, crevices pull apart, and rumbling earth makes every footstep perilous for the enemy while wide paths are carved for the friends of Orboros.

While in Baldur's control area, friendly models gain cover. While in Baldur's control area, enemy models never have Pathfinder and treat open terrain as rough terrain. Broken Earth lasts for one round.

BALDUR

🌀 **Pathfinder**

Elemental Mastery – Warbeasts in this model's battlegroup with Construct 🔁 beginning their activations in this model's control area can charge and make power attacks without being forced. This model can heal friendly warbeasts in its battlegroup that have Construct 🔁.

Forest Walk – While completely within a forest, this model can forfeit its normal movement to use Forest Walk. If it does, choose a location completely within this model's control area that is completely within a forest. Remove this model from the forest and place it in the chosen location. This model cannot use Forest Walk while knocked down.

TRITUS

⊘ **Magical Weapon**

🔁 **Reach**

Weight of Stone – When a model is damaged by this weapon it suffers –3 SPD and DEF for one round.

SPELLS	COST	RNG	AOE	POW	UP	OFF
EARTH SPIKES	3	10	3	13	NO	YES

When making this attack, ignore cover and the +2 DEF bonus for elevation. On a critical hit, models hit are knocked down.

SPELLS	COST	RNG	AOE	POW	UP	OFF
RAPID GROWTH	2	CTRL	4	–	YES	NO

Place the AOE completely in this model's control area. The AOE is a forest that remains in play as long as upkeep is paid.

SPELLS	COST	RNG	AOE	POW	UP	OFF
SOLID GROUND	2	SELF	CTRL	–	YES	NO

While in this model's control area, friendly models cannot be knocked down and do not suffer blast damage.

SPELLS	COST	RNG	AOE	POW	UP	OFF
STONE SKIN	2	6	–	–	YES	NO

Target friendly Faction model/unit gains +2 STR and ARM but suffers –1 SPD and DEF.

Older than he appears, Baldur has overseen numerous territories in his tenure with the Circle, has mentored powerful younger druids like Kaya the Wildborne, and has established unusual friendships with outsiders. He cares nothing for druidic politics and reserves his philosophy for the shaping of stone; he has shared lore with Rhulic stonemasons and even conducted terse exchanges with the guardians of Ios. In better days he was a welcome guest among kriels of the Thornwood and Scarsfell, and he considers the rift with the trollkin to be disappointing, even as he will not shirk from his duty to battle them. His logical and insightful appeals give him a powerful voice among the ranks of the Circle. His promotion to potent continued his gradual rise through the ranks, and he has been entrusted with the deeper mysteries of druidic lore.

The Stonecleaver is a paragon of the earth-shaping path of druidic magic: he deeply understands stone, earth, and the forest; he has mastered the shaping of wolds and their ilk; and he can infuse primal power into stone runes. His thick fingers possess the skill and artistry of a sculptor, but his masterpieces spring to life and stride onto the battlefield to tear walls and beasts asunder. Baldur's magic enlivens forests in even the most blighted places, and he uses these trees to cross enormous distances and pulverize the enemies of the Circle Orboros.

Everblight's menace weighs heavily on Baldur's mind. The dragon's unnatural blight warps all it touches, leaving scars that will never heal. The Stonecleaver has slept little since the rise of this threat, waking each morning before sunrise to work on a warden or muster for battle. Baldur has spent considerable time patrolling the wilds of northern Khador, slicing into the forward elements of the encroaching Legion. Despite all these dire omens, however, Baldur somehow remains optimistic about the future—a beacon of energy and vitality who insists no fight is lost until all will is lost.

A bastion of strength and resolve noted for his steadfast loyalty, Baldur the Stonecleaver is described among the Circle as the "Rock of Orboros." Some jest he has spent too long communing with mountains, for he is a calm and serene presence among his more passionate peers. When his battle temper is aroused, however, he becomes an unstoppable juggernaut made flesh.

Baldur laughs off questions about his past, saying he was born in a bear cave near Boarsgate, but there is an undeniably Khardic flavor to his features and hulking frame. He moves with deceptive ease as strength flows into him from the earth. His massive stone sword sings through the air and shatters anything it encounters. No other man has ever been able to lift this weapon, let alone wield it in battle. Baldur insists this has nothing to do with strength of limb but is because the sword is as much a part of him as his arms.

CASSIUS THE OATHKEEPER & WURMWOOD, TREE OF FATE
CIRCLE WARLOCK & CHARACTER SOLO

I seal the Oath with my blood, my life. I am nothing before Orboros.

—The final words of the Oath

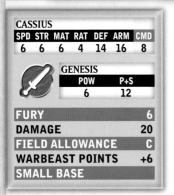

CASSIUS						
SPD	STR	MAT	RAT	DEF	ARM	CMD
6	6	6	4	14	16	8

GENESIS		
	POW	P+S
	6	12

FURY	6
DAMAGE	20
FIELD ALLOWANCE	C
WARBEAST POINTS	+6
SMALL BASE	

FEAT: FOREST OF JUDGMENT

Cassius the Oathkeeper can call forth the final judgment of Wurmwood to reap a harvest of offerings and soothe the scarred body of Orboros. The ancient tree erupts from the earth with a profusion of blood-starved branches, as sharp as spears and eager to feast on those who are delivered into their deadly embrace.

Wurmwood, Tree of Fate's command range becomes a forest. Enemy models that are knocked down while in Wurmwood's command range suffer 1 damage point. Forest of Judgment lasts for one round.

CASSIUS

 Pathfinder

Black Roots – This model ignores the firing into melee penalty when making magic attacks against models in Wurmwood's command range.

Treewalker – This model ignores forests when determining LOS. While in a forest, this model gains +2 DEF against melee attack rolls and can advance through obstructions and other models if it has enough movement to move completely past them.

GENESIS

Magical Weapon

Reach

Fertilizer – When a living or undead model is boxed by this weapon, center a 3" AOE on it and then remove the model from play. The AOE is a forest that remains in play for one round.

SPELLS	COST	RNG	AOE	POW	UP	OFF
CURSE OF SHADOWS	3	8	–	–	YES	YES

Target model/unit suffers –2 ARM and cannot make free strikes. A model can advance through an affected model if it has enough movement to move completely past its base.

HELLMOUTH	4	8	*	12	NO	YES

If this attack misses, nothing happens. If it hits, before making the damage roll, push models within 3" of the model hit 3" directly toward it in the order you choose. Then center a 3" AOE on the model hit. Models hit suffer a POW 12 damage roll. Models boxed by Hellmouth are removed from play.

STRANGLEHOLD	2	10	–	11	NO	YES

A model damaged by Stranglehold forfeits either its movement or its action during its next activation, as its controller chooses.

UNSEEN PATH	2	CTRL	–	–	NO	NO

Unseen Path can be cast only while Wurmwood, Tree of Fate is in this model's control area. When Unseen Path is cast, immediately place this model within 2" of Wurmwood or place Wurmwood within 2" of this model. A model cannot advance this turn after being placed by Unseen Path.

TACTICAL TIPS

FERTILIZER – Because the boxed model is removed from play before being destroyed, it does not generate a soul or corpse token.

HELLMOUTH – Boxed models do not provide soul or corpse tokens.

The druids of the Circle Orboros have made countless alliances, manipulations, and bargains to ensure the primacy of their agendas, but some of these have been more lasting than others. The first omnipotents of the Circle sealed ominous bargains with manifestations of Orboros given form on Caen, entities like the Lord of Feasts and Wurmwood, also called the Tree of Fate. These primal entities proved to be formidable but demanding allies.

Before Menoth gave man the first laws and taught them to erect the first walls, the carnivorous tree named Wurmwood had taken root. Unlike most trees, it was thirsty for blood and quickly manifested an unusually deep and predatory intelligence. The first druids of the Circle used their influence to persuade Devourer cultists to conduct sacrifices below the spread of its branches. The scattered tribes of the hinterlands traveled great distances to pour libations of blood upon the soil above its roots and hang skeletal offerings from its leafless limbs. These terrible rites culminated in a great ritual wherein thousands of men and beasts were bled out to give the tree a feast worthy of the Unsleeping One. Unfettered powers of creation thrummed in the air as a single root burst forth to entwine itself about a young druid through which the tree spoke its name. This rite enabled Wurmwood to communicate through a human voice. In this first communion a lasting pact was sealed with the Circle Orboros.

Only the omnipotents know the exact words of this agreement, but since that time in every age one druid must uphold a special covenant with the Tree of Fate. This druid gives over life and soul to become a conduit between Wurmwood and the human masters of the Circle Orboros. Wurmwood's unfathomable mind does not perceive Caen or the passage of time as mortals do and so requires an intermediary.

Effortlessly tapping into the natural energies of Orboros below the skin of the world, the tree comes and goes at its whim. Though it appears to be permanently rooted, it can disappear in a shimmer of fog to manifest elsewhere. For generations Wurmwood has made its home in various dark forest hearts and on remote mountains. Devourer cultists seek it out to nourish their primal god with the blood of sacrifices. The ranking druids of the Circle periodically offer their own supplications in exchange for its wisdom. Wurmwood is invited to attend the most

TACTICAL TIPS

ALTAR OF SACRIFICE – Cassius the Oathkeeper can exceed his FURY stat in fury points as a result of Altar of Sacrifice.

IMMOBILE – This model can be placed.

guarded Circle deliberations, where it has special privilege. When the omnipotents cannot agree upon a course of action, Wurmwood is empowered to draw upon its unique perspective to discern the best path.

Mortal flesh ages, and when the time comes for Wurmwood to choose a new conduit, the potents gather their fresh wilders. These are chosen for their youth, stamina, and potency in the mystic arts. Being selected for this group is a dubious and unwelcome honor, for it carries a terrible burden. Leading druids often arrange for favored subordinates to be absent from the selection ceremony. On the night of Geremor's Feast, Wurmwood casts aside the aging druid previously chosen, his life extinguished. At the same moment Wurmwood's roots entwine around its selected candidate, who must speak the ancient words of the oath or risk being crushed. Once this vow is completed, the tree consumes the druid's memories and integrates itself into his flesh.

The druid's personality lingers beyond this joining; each generation, the tree's perspective is colored by the mind of its conduit. Cassius, the current chosen, was a cunning and intuitive druid who earned the jealous ire of his master over some perceived affront. The old master thought this slight avenged when Wurmwood selected his troublesome apprentice, but this satisfaction was short-lived. This mentor was soon forgotten, while Cassius persists as part of an immortal entity that manifests the will of Orboros. Perhaps from the influence of Cassius, Wurmwood has become increasingly active in recent decades. The tree and its conduit manifest at times and places of their choosing where they obliterate all opposition and bring swift victory to the Circle Orboros.

Though the tree accepts any sacrifices, it thrives best on the blood and souls of its enemies. The war hosts it leads seem to become particularly vicious when it urges them onward. The Tree of Fate appears where it deigns and in every conflict judges the worth of the fallen, allies and enemies alike, as it soaks its roots in their gore. Its violence suggests the end awaiting all things should the Devourer fully awaken.

WURMWOOD
⬤ Advance Deployment

WURMWOOD						
SPD	STR	MAT	RAT	DEF	ARM	CMD
0	0	0	0	5	16	10

FIELD ALLOWANCE	C
LARGE BASE	

Altar of Sacrifice – This model gains one soul token for each living model destroyed in its command range. This model can have up to five soul tokens at a time. If this model is in Cassius the Oathkeeper's control area at the start of his activation, at that time Cassius can remove soul tokens from it to put fury on himself at 1 fury point per soul token removed.

Companion [Cassius the Oathkeeper] – This model is included in any army that includes Cassius the Oathkeeper. If Cassius is destroyed or removed from play, remove this model from play. This model is part of Cassius' battlegroup.

Ghost Shield – This model gains +1 ARM for each soul token currently on it.

Immobile – This model has no movement or action and cannot be knocked down or moved. Its front arc extends to 360°. It has no melee range, cannot engage, and is automatically hit by melee attacks.

Prowl – This model gains Stealth (⬤) while within terrain that provides concealment, the AOE of a spell that provides concealment, or the AOE of a cloud effect.

Sympathetic Link – When this model would suffer damage, you must assign that damage to Cassius the Oathkeeper. This model does not suffer the damage assigned to Cassius. This damage can be transferred.

KAYA THE WILDBORNE
CIRCLE WARLOCK

She is bold, courageous, and utterly committed to Orboros. Kaya's spirit is untamed and embodies what is best among us.

—Baldur the Stonecleaver

KAYA						
SPD	STR	MAT	RAT	DEF	ARM	CMD
7	5	6	4	16	13	8

SPLINTER		
	POW	P+S
	6	11

FURY	6
DAMAGE	16
FIELD ALLOWANCE	C
WARBEAST POINTS	+6
SMALL BASE	

FEAT: WILD MASTERY

The wilding removes a druid from the rest of humanity, opens a primeval conduit to forgotten powers, and enables communion with beasts. Kaya the Wildborne endured a wilding so intense it has left her with unrivaled mastery of her feral warbeasts. She can unleash a surge of rage in any nearby warbeast and siphon this ferocity to lend the bestial strength to her own power.

Place up to 3 fury points on each friendly Faction warbeast in Kaya's battlegroup that is in her control area. She can immediately leach fury points from warbeasts in her battlegroup in her control area.

KAYA

🐾 Pathfinder

Pack Hunters – Living warbeasts in this model's battlegroup in its control area gain +2 on melee attack rolls.

SPLINTER

⚙ Magical Weapon

➹ Reach

Critical Knockdown – On a critical hit, the model hit is knocked down.

SPELLS	COST	RNG	AOE	POW	UP	OFF
OCCULTATION	2	6	-	-	YES	NO
Target friendly model/unit gains Stealth ⚑.						
SOOTHING SONG	1	SELF	CTRL	-	NO	NO
Remove up to 1 fury point from each friendly living Faction warbeast currently in this model's control area. Soothing Song can only be cast once per turn.						
SPIRIT DOOR	3	CTRL	-	-	NO	NO
Select a model in this model's battlegroup in its control area. If this model is selected, immediately place it within 2″ of another model in its battlegroup that was in its control area at the time the spell was cast. If another model in this model's battlegroup is selected, immediately place that model within 2″ of this model. A model cannot advance or attack after being placed by Spirit Door this turn.						
SPIRIT FANG	2	10	-	12	NO	YES
A model damaged by Spirit Fang suffers −2 SPD and DEF for one round.						

TACTICAL TIPS

WILD MASTERY – Because Kaya is leaching these fury points, her fury point total cannot exceed her current FURY as a result of Wild Mastery.

Kaya the Wildborne plunges herself into the minds of beasts with an abandon unequalled among her peers. While riding this tide she is a ruthless and savage creature who tirelessly stalks her prey day or night. When she enters this battle trance there is no future and no past, only the infinite present and the sweet promise of blood.

Her willingness to submerge herself so deeply into the consciousness of her pack worries her mentor Baldur the Stonecleaver, yet it seems inseparable from her nature. Older druids have tried to teach her patience, but she chafes at their inability to understand her way. For Kaya more than any druid in recent memory, the *wilding* was no struggle but an awakening of her true self. She throws herself into battles with ardent courage without worrying about her own preservation. This irrepressible spirit has led to victory after victory and provided unexpected windfalls to the Circle Orboros.

Though she does not remember her early life, Kaya was born in eastern Ord within sight of the Thornwood Forest. She felt the wilding as a toddler and distressed her parents in the middle of the night on Calder's full moon by shrieking out her window. Even more alarming were the answering howls of wolves. Perhaps it was with relief that they handed their peculiar daughter to the hulking blackclad stranger who came knocking on their door. Since that day, Baldur has been the only father Kaya has ever known. Though her path has taken her elsewhere, she always returns for advice, and he remains the only ranking druid she trusts implicitly.

Kaya believes other Circle leaders are needlessly manipulative, and she rarely agrees with their decisions. She has no ability to govern her tongue and has insulted many of her peers without even knowing it. This may result from so much time spent in the minds of beasts who do not dissemble, lie, or understand tact.

For similar reasons, Kaya does not participate in the schemes and plots for which the druids are famed. She finds the motivations of beasts more to her liking, as they require only food, shelter, and a strong will to lead them. Kaya prefers to let her actions speak for themselves as she strikes even harder against the enemies of the Circle, and her recent effectiveness in numerous engagements against Everblight's Legion has won her some respect.

Though capable of sacrificing them if the need is great, Kaya has a tight bond with her beasts and is able to inspire in them remarkable efforts. Their loyalty to her is genuine. Her piercing eyes contain the cold, hard stare of a battlefield veteran twice her age, and with the merest glance she conveys that she has experienced her share of horrors and intends to do her part to end them.

KAYA THE MOONHUNTER & LARIS
CIRCLE EPIC WARLOCK & CIRCLE CHARACTER LIGHT WARBEAST

Despite all attempts to shelter and control her, this one's destiny blazes with the power of the unconquered sun.

—Krueger the Stormlord

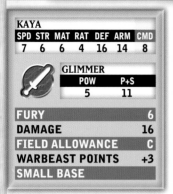

KAYA						
SPD	STR	MAT	RAT	DEF	ARM	CMD
7	6	6	4	16	14	8

GLIMMER		
	POW	P+S
	5	11

FURY	6
DAMAGE	16
FIELD ALLOWANCE	C
WARBEAST POINTS	+3
SMALL BASE	

FEAT: CALL OF THE HUNT

Kaya the Moonhunter can immerse herself in the minds of her beasts to fuse their efforts into a single flawless execution of her will and unleash them in a seemingly reckless assault to rend and kill anything they find. Calling on ancient rites, Kaya can then instantly summon her companions back to her side to stand watchful vigil.

Kaya can force warbeasts in her battlegroup even if they are outside her control area. At the end of the activation of each warbeast in her battlegroup, you can place that warbeast anywhere within 3″ of Kaya. Call of the Hunt lasts for one turn.

KAYA
🌒 **Pathfinder**

Alpha – Living warbeasts in this model's battlegroup beginning their activation in its control area can run, charge, or make a slam or trample power attack without being forced.

Flank [faction warbeast] – When this model makes a melee attack against an enemy model within the melee range of a friendly model of the type indicated, this model gains +2 to attack rolls and gains an additional damage die.

Unyielding – While engaging an enemy model, this model gains +2 ARM.

GLIMMER
⚔ **Magical Weapon**
🗡 **Reach**

SPELLS	COST	RNG	AOE	POW	UP	OFF
DOG PILE	2	10	-	-	YES	YES

Warbeasts in this model's battlegroup can charge or make slam power attacks against target enemy model without being forced and regardless of LOS. When a warbeast does, it gains +2″ movement and gains Pathfinder 🌒 while resolving that charge or slam.

FORCED EVOLUTION	2	6	-	-	YES	NO

Target friendly living Faction warbeast gains +2 STR and DEF.

MUZZLE	2	10	-	12	NO	YES

An enemy warbeast damaged by Muzzle cannot advance toward this model for one round.

SHADOW PACK	3	SELF	CTRL	-	YES	NO

Models in this model's battlegroup gain Stealth 🦉 while in its control area.

TACTICAL TIPS

DOG PILE – Modifiers to movement apply only to a model's normal movement.

Countless battles have honed Kaya to perfect fighting form, proving repeatedly she has the will and strength to survive against impossible odds. She fights with a visceral joy for the rush of battle but also with a determined belief that her enemies deserve destruction. Her clarity of purpose springs from the same wild spirit that allows her effortlessly to control the beasts accompanying her, including the great wolf Laris who keeps constant vigil at her side. She stands on the precipice of greatness and has proven her willingness to leap into the unknown— regardless of the dangers—to seize it.

Laris is a creature as preternatural as he is wild, a cunning and adaptive reflection of some inner portion of Kaya's predatory spirit. He is the answer to Kaya's call for the other half of herself, and the bond between them is essential and profound. The link that joins their minds and emotions allow them to accomplish otherwise impossible feats. Kaya's power flows naturally through Laris, and

Laris feels her wounds more keenly than injury to his own flesh. Outside of battle his mind is a soothing influence on Kaya's inner turmoil, and his instinct to preserve her life perfectly contrasts her sometimes reckless courage. He is a manifestation of Orboros with a wisdom and personality all his own.

Connecting to Laris was no simple feat, requiring Kaya to stretch in a way she never had before. One key to unlocking this deeper power was learning the role of celestial influences empowering the Circle Orboros. Under the tutelage of Morvahna the Autumnblade she began to tap into the moons' mystical pull on the blood of all predators. Morvahna initiated Kaya into these elder rites by urging her to undertake a strenuous ordeal: climbing to one of the highest peaks in the Wyrmwall Mountains to unlock her inner strength and predatory awareness.

Atop the mountain peaks she arrived at a nearly forgotten sacrificial site. She spilled her blood on ancient stones as lightning crackled across the storm-tossed sky. Then the black clouds parted and the three moons of Caen illuminated the tableau. She was startled and awed when a ghostly white wolf emerged from the wilds at the ritual's climax. With a single look, Kaya knew the wolf's mind and could sense its greeting. He invited her to hunt, and as she joined the wolf in a run through the mountain passes the two bonded inextricably.

She named him Laris after the second of the moons orbiting Caen. The ignorant call this moon baleful and wicked, and it is associated with storms and ill fortune. Laris has in fact proven to be a calming influence on the beasts accompanying Kaya into battle. Through the bond

ANIMUS	COST	RNG	AOE	POW	UP	OFF
SPIRIT SHIFT	2	SELF	–	–	NO	NO

When this model uses Spirit Shift, immediately place it within 2″ of Kaya. When Kaya uses Spirit Shift, immediately place her within 2″ of this model. A model cannot advance this turn after being placed by Spirit Shift.

LARIS

 Pathfinder

LARIS						
SPD	STR	MAT	RAT	DEF	ARM	CMD
7	8	6	4	15	14	7

BITE		
H	POW	P+S
	4	12

FURY	3
THRESHOLD	10
FIELD ALLOWANCE	C
MEDIUM BASE	

Companion [Kaya the Moonhunter] – This model is included in any army that includes Kaya the Moonhunter. If Kaya is destroyed or removed from play, remove this model from play. This model is part of Kaya's battlegroup.

Guard Dog – While this model is within 3″ of its warcaster or warlock and is not knocked down or stationary, its warcaster or warlock cannot be targeted by free strikes and gains +2 DEF against melee attack rolls, and models attacking the warcaster or warlock do not gain back strike bonuses.

Warbeast Bond [Kaya the Moonhunter] – Laris is bonded to Kaya the Moonhunter. If Laris frenzies, he cannot choose Kaya as his target. While Laris is in Kaya's control area, she can channel spells through him.

they share, Kaya can feel the complex flow of his emotions and thoughts, receiving warnings and sometimes seeing through his eyes. Laris does not filter the world through language but boasts a keen perception and insight. He is an accomplished hunter and a brave guardian. Though Kaya has become calmer since bonding with him, the cold predatory stare of a wolf sometimes shines in her eyes. A wolf feels no sorrow or compassion for its prey, and Kaya has put aside such human feelings, knowing hesitation could mean death in battle.

When Kaya descended the mountain and met again with the Autumnblade, the senior druid was surprised and unsettled by the way her protégé had exceeded her expectations. The appearance of the wolf showed that Kaya had transcended the mentorship of elder druids.

Kaya has learned from hard experience that some of her peers will try to exploit her potential for their own benefit. Over time her confidence has grown, she has learned how to put her power to use without becoming the tool of another, and she has refined her instincts. Once she moved from one battle to the next without thought beyond the moment. She has learned to transcend this, mastering deeper rites and rituals from the lore of beast masters who preceded her. The more Kaya learns, the more she appreciates the solid foundation given to her by Baldur the Stonecleaver. She intends to heed Baldur's example by focusing squarely on the enemy and ignoring all other distractions.

The soil of countless wild places in western Immoren has tasted the blood of Kaya's enemies. In battle she moves with fluid grace and amazing speed and relishes being surrounded by foes. As Kaya leaps into the midst of her enemies, warpwolves, satyrs, and Laris suddenly appear from the shadows of trees, their limbs infused with vitality. Never has carnage achieved such sublime perfection as when Kaya and her beasts unleash themselves, holding nothing in reserve as they seek to scatter the enemy shattered and bleeding across the forest soil.

KROMAC THE RAVENOUS
CIRCLE THARN WARLOCK

He stepped from the battle, washed head to toe with gore. As Kromac passed, I saw the Lord of the Feast bow to him as a servant would to his master.

—Huntsman Garkarsh Martovin

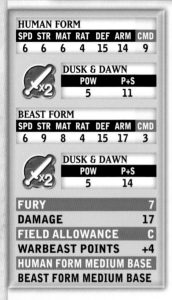

HUMAN FORM						
SPD	STR	MAT	RAT	DEF	ARM	CMD
6	6	6	4	15	14	9

DUSK & DAWN		
	POW	P+S
⚔️ ×2	5	11

BEAST FORM						
SPD	STR	MAT	RAT	DEF	ARM	CMD
6	9	8	4	15	17	3

DUSK & DAWN		
	POW	P+S
⚔️ ×2	5	14

FURY	7
DAMAGE	17
FIELD ALLOWANCE	C
WARBEAST POINTS	+4
HUMAN FORM MEDIUM BASE	
BEAST FORM MEDIUM BASE	

FEAT: BLOOD RAGE

Kromac the Ravenous is the inheritor of ancient and fell magics. In times of need he can feast upon his own essence as he devours the blood and hearts of his vanquished foes.

Kromac suffers up to 7 damage points. For each damage point he suffers, Kromac gains 1 fury point. Kromac's fury point total cannot exceed his current FURY as a result of Blood Rage. If Kromac is in human form when this feat is used, he can immediately take beast form; replace his human model with his beast model. Effects on the replaced model are applied to the beast model.

HUMAN FORM

🌑 **Pathfinder**

Altered States – At the start of your Maintenance Phase, choose a form for this model to take: human or beast. If it changes form, replace the model in play with its alternate form. Effects on the replaced model are applied to the alternate form. You decide which form this model starts the game in.

Beast Out – When this model suffers damage from an enemy attack during an opponent's turn while in human form, immediately after the attack is resolved this model can spend 1 fury point to take beast form. Replace its human model with the beast model. Effects on the replaced model are applied to the beast model.

BEAST FORM

🌑 **Pathfinder**

⊗ **Terror**

Altered States – See above.

Beast Mind – This model cannot upkeep spells and cannot cast non-animus spells.

Jump – After using its normal movement to make a full advance but before performing an action, you can place this model anywhere completely within 5″ of its current location. Any effects that prevent it from charging also prevent it from using Jump.

DUSK & DAWN

⊘ **Magical Weapon**

⊘ **Reach**

Kromac the Ravenous is a barbarian king and warlord of his people. When he walks as a man, silence surrounds him as gathered Tharn await his command for the chance to kill or die as he wills. When Kromac draws upon the Wurm to transform into a beast, wild things hear his howl and leap

SPELLS	COST	RNG	AOE	POW	UP	OFF
BESTIAL	3	SELF	CTRL	–	NO	NO

While in this model's control area, enemy models cannot cast spells or be used to channel spells. Bestial lasts for one round.

INVIOLABLE RESOLVE	2	6	–	–	YES	NO

Target friendly Faction model/unit gains +2 ARM and Fearless ✠.

RIFT	3	8	4	13	NO	YES

The AOE is rough terrain and remains in play for one round.

WARPATH	2	SELF	CTRL	–	YES	NO

When a friendly Faction model in this model's control area destroys one or more enemy models with a melee or ranged attack during its activation, immediately after the attack is resolved, one warbeast in this model's battlegroup that is in its control area can advance up to 3″. A warbeast can advance only once per turn as a result of Warpath.

WILD AGGRESSION	3	6	–	–	YES	NO

Target friendly living warbeast in this model's battlegroup can run, charge, or make slam or trample power attacks without being forced and gains boosted melee attack rolls.

TACTICAL TIPS

INVIOLABLE RESOLVE – Fleeing models that gain Fearless immediately rally.

to obey. From the deepest heart of the black wilderness he comes seeking not conquest but slaughter and destruction. The druids of the Circle Orboros do not count him among their number but consider him a sword wielded only reluctantly, one not easily sheathed once drawn.

Something has always set Kromac apart from other Tharn. The wind whispered words only he could hear, and the howls of wolves resonated in his heart even when he walked as a man. He took the path of the shaman and learned the blood rites of sacrifice, but something within him knew there was more to learn. Kromac had, in fact, been born with the wilding—unheard-of among Tharn.

Krueger the Stormlord, once called "Storm Father" by the Tharn, came to Kromac and instructed him in the use of this power. The wilding combined with the Tharn gifts and brought forth wild savagery and strength beyond any of his people, yet this came at the price of reason. Kromac entered the beast-mind when he transformed and became the walking death, an avatar of slaughter with axes in his hands. This transformation's price is a form of wild madness that unlocks the most primal essence of the predatory spirit.

The Stormlord remains one of the few humans Kromac truly respects. Kromac's unique power drew the attention of another great druid who would first earn, and eventually betray, his loyalty. Decades ago Kromac witnessed firsthand as Morvahna the Autumnblade played the key role in breaking the Curse of the Ten Ills that afflicted his people. He viewed Morvahna with a complex mix of awe, lust, and deeper longing that unsettled him, for he saw her as the salvation of his race and an immortal vision of female perfection.

For years he served Morvahna and watched his people return to strength, but eventually her disregard for Tharn lives and her willingness to use him as a tool forced Kromac to see her with fresh eyes. Kromac recently turned his back on Morvahna and returned to the service of his old mentor, who welcomed him as a vital asset. Kromac knows he was born to embody destruction and slaughter, and he has much work to do in the days ahead.

KRUEGER THE STORMWRATH
CIRCLE WARLOCK

To understand Krueger you must think of him not as a man but as a force of nature. He is the raging hurricane, the wild tornado obliterating anything in its path and leaving others to pick up the pieces.
—Omnipotent Lortus

KRUEGER						
SPD	STR	MAT	RAT	DEF	ARM	CMD
6	5	5	6	15	14	8

LIGHTNING			
RNG	ROF	AOE	POW
10	1	—	13

LIGHTNING SPEAR	
POW	P+S
7	12

FURY	7
DAMAGE	16
FIELD ALLOWANCE	C
WARBEAST POINTS	+5
SMALL BASE	

FEAT: STORM RAVAGER

This is the Stormwrath. All despair when the sky shouts its verdict of thunderous doom and death by lightning's spear.

Place three 3" AOEs anywhere completely in Krueger's control area. Enemy models in one or more of the AOEs when they are placed suffer a boostable POW 10 electrical damage roll ⚡. During each of your Maintenance Phases, remove one AOE. An enemy model entering or ending its activation in one or more AOEs suffers an unboostable POW 10 electrical damage roll.

KRUEGER

⊘ **Immunity: Electricity**

🌀 **Pathfinder**

LIGHTNING

⚡ **Damage Type: Electricity**

⊘ **Magical Weapon**

Electro Leap – When a model is hit with this weapon, you can have lightning arc to the nearest model within 4" of the model hit, ignoring the attacking model. The model the lightning arcs to suffers an unboostable POW 10 electrical damage roll ⚡.

LIGHTNING SPEAR

⊘ **Magical Weapon**

⊘ **Reach**

Sustained Attack – During this model's activation, when it makes an attack with this weapon against the last model hit by the weapon this activation, the attack automatically hits.

SPELLS	COST	RNG	AOE	POW	UP	OFF
CHAIN LIGHTNING	3	10	–	10	NO	YES

A model hit by Chain Lightning suffers a POW 10 electrical damage roll ⚡, and lightning arcs from that model to d6 consecutive additional models. The lightning arcs to the nearest model it has not already arced to within 4" of the last model it arced to, ignoring this model. Each model the lightning arcs to suffers a POW 10 electrical damage roll ⚡.

DEFLECTION	2	SELF	CTRL	–	NO	NO

While in this model's control area, friendly Faction warrior models gain +2 ARM against ranged and magic attack damage rolls. Deflection lasts for one round.

LIGHTNING TENDRILS	3	6	–	–	YES	NO

Target friendly model/unit gains Immunity: Electricity ⊘. Affected model's melee weapons gain Reach ⊘ and Electro Leap. (When a model is hit by a weapon with Electro Leap, you can have lightning arc to the nearest model within 4" of the model hit, ignoring the attacking model. The model the lightning arcs to suffers an unboostable POW 10 electrical damage roll ⚡.)

SKYBORNE	2	SELF	–	–	NO	NO

This model gains +2 SPD and DEF and Flight for one round. (A model with Flight can advance through terrain and obstacles without penalty and can advance through obstructions and other models if it has enough movement to move completely past them. It ignores intervening models when declaring its charge target.)

TORNADO	4	10	–	13	NO	YES

Instead of suffering a normal damage roll, a non-incorporeal model hit by Tornado is thrown d6" directly away from the spell's point of origin regardless of its base size and suffers a POW 13 damage roll. Collateral damage from this throw is POW 13.

TACTICAL TIPS

ELECTRO LEAP – The lightning will still arc to a model with Immunity: Electricity; it just cannot damage that model. Damage from Electro Leap is not considered to have been caused by a hit or by a melee or ranged attack.

CHAIN LIGHTNING – The lightning can arc to models with Immunity: Electricity; it just cannot damage them. Damage from Chain Lightning strikes is magic damage and is not considered to have been caused by a hit.

TORNADO – Incorporeal models are not thrown; they just suffer a damage roll.

Universally feared, respected, and disliked within the Circle hierarchy, Krueger the Stormwrath counts no man as friend and no druid his equal. He earned his name by performing deeds such as climbing atop the highest Watcher Peak and calling down a storm powerful enough to raise the waters of Lake Rimmocksdale and nearly drown the city of Orven. The Stormwrath was the only witness to the death of Omnipotent Ergonus, and he seethes at the promotion of Lortus to fill that vacant leadership position. Convinced he is being punished for surviving the battle that took Ergonus' life, Krueger longs to reach the pinnacle of authority so that he can assert his will over the Circle. Krueger believes the blackclads have become too soft and require his guidance to return to the days of plague and flood.

Born in a small village north of Sul, Krueger is among the few to have survived a wilding in the Protectorate of Menoth. The firstborn of a Menite priest, Krueger was quickly condemned when he began manifesting his strange gift. Proclaiming him a spawn of the Devourer, Krueger's father tied him to a stake and prepared to burn him alive. Druids of the Circle had been observing young Krueger for some time, however, and intervened with bloody swiftness. They took the boy to a hidden dwelling near the ruins of Acrennia to be tutored by Mohsar the Desertwalker, a harsh master renowned for teaching the power of desert and ocean by cruel example. He once stripped Krueger and abandoned him in the desert hills east of Acrennia, forcing him to return using his own strength and cunning.

Krueger delights in bringing suffering to the cities of men. He would shatter the walls of Sul and Caspia and drive the inhabitants of both cities out into the gulf to drown. The Stormwrath holds a particular scorn for Menoth and hopes to wipe all trace of the god's despicable sycophants from the face of Caen. Baptized in the blood of Menites, Krueger's great spear contains the Tongue of the Wurm, an endless lightning storm held captive in the heart of its wooden shaft.

Krueger revels in the Devourer more than his peers, seeing no meaningful difference between the Wurm and Orboros.

He has attended the savage rites of the Tharn and other berserker tribes on the fringes of humanity, offering human sacrifices on druid stones and standing awash in blood to gnaw on the hearts of the slain. Krueger fully embraces the destructive energies he has learned to unleash.

The Stormwrath rides a constant wave of barely restrained fury visible to anyone brave enough to look into his eyes. His deep and unquenchable rage will be satisfied only when every institution of civilized man lies crumbled, burned, or drowned at his feet.

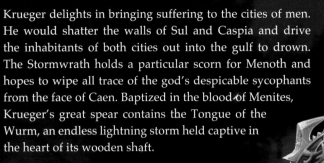

KRUEGER THE STORMLORD
CIRCLE EPIC WARLOCK

With knowledge and power illimitable, it is inexcusable that this order remains content to stand idly as the world crumbles.

—Krueger the Stormlord

KRUEGER						
SPD	STR	MAT	RAT	DEF	ARM	CMD
6	5	6	6	15	15	9

LIGHTNING BOLT			
RNG	ROF	AOE	POW
10	3	–	12

WURMTONGUE	
POW	P+S
7	12

Rules SPACER

FURY	7
DAMAGE	16
FIELD ALLOWANCE	C
WARBEAST POINTS	+5
SMALL BASE	

FEAT: HURRICANE

The air itself bows to Krueger's will. In the blink of an eye even the stillest calm becomes a raging hurricane. Enemies are powerless to advance against the howling wind. They labor for every inch they gain as they suffer the Stormlord's fury.

Enemy models currently in Krueger's control area are pushed 3″ directly away from Krueger and suffer −2 SPD for one round. You determine the order models are moved.

KRUEGER

⊗ **Immunity: Electricity**

Flight – This model can advance through terrain and obstacles without penalty and can advance through obstructions and other models if it has enough movement to move completely past them. This model ignores intervening models when declaring its charge target.

Inspiration [Circle] – Friendly Circle models/units in this model's command range never flee and immediately rally.

LIGHTNING BOLT

⚡ **Damage Type: Electricity**

⊘ **Magical Weapon**

Sustained Attack – During this model's activation, when it makes an attack with this weapon against the last model hit by the weapon this activation, the attack automatically hits.

WURMTONGUE

⊘ **Magical Weapon**

⊘ **Reach**

Disruption – A warjack hit loses its focus points and cannot be allocated focus or channel spells for one round.

SPELLS	COST	RNG	AOE	POW	UP	OFF
GALLOWS	3	10	–	13	NO	YES

When an enemy model is hit by this attack, it can be pushed d6″ directly toward Gallows' point of origin.

LIGHTNING STORM	3	8	3	10	NO	YES

Models hit suffer a POW 10 electrical damage ⚡ roll. The AOE remains in play for one round. Models entering or ending their activations in the AOE suffer a POW 10 electrical damage ⚡ roll.

STORM WALL	3	SELF	CTRL	–	NO	NO

While in this model's control area, enemy models suffer −5 RNG on their ranged attacks. When an enemy AOE ranged attack deviates from a point in this model's control area, after determining the deviation distance, you choose the direction the AOE deviates. Storm Wall lasts for one round.

TELEKINESIS	2	8	–	–	NO	*

Place target model completely within 2″ of its current location. When Telekinesis targets an enemy model, it is an offensive spell and requires a magic attack roll. A model can be affected by Telekinesis only once per turn.

TACTICAL TIPS

HURRICANE – If a model's SPD is reduced for any reason, it cannot charge or make slam or trample power attacks.

GALLOWS – This means the model is moved before it suffers damage.

It was after he came to the aid of Kromac the Ravenous in the Thornwood that Krueger began to realize how limited his perspective had become. How could he grasp the greater situation when tied down to meaningless errands and petty scheming? He knows now the omnipotents' game is to sit in the background spinning their spider webs while keeping their subordinates ignorant of the deeper follies into which the Circle has tumbled.

Krueger believes himself to be the only man who can make a lasting change in the world. He will take the steps the rest of his peers are too cowardly to attempt. The Stormlord proved his audacity after he decided his order had been complacent about the dragons corrupting Orboros. Rather than seeking to confront Everblight, Krueger defied the omnipotents' orders and brought the matter before another dragon. Blighterghast listened to Krueger describe the threat Everblight represents to the dragon alliance against Lord Toruk, prompting other members of that alliance to stir again for the first time in centuries. Krueger considers the disaster and widespread destruction that may come of this a necessary price, for he believes the aftermath will allow them to strike the first significant blow against civilization in his order's long history. The only question is whether the Circle can survive the coming storm to see their ultimate goal fulfilled.

Even the three omnipotents of the Circle Orboros admit Krueger is among the most powerful of their order. He furthermore has the vision to apprehend that greatness does not come as a reward for humility or dedication. He intends to rattle the Circle Orboros like a rickety house caught in a storm. If he makes enemies of the most powerful individuals in western Immoren in the process, so be it.

Krueger lost patience with the omnipotents after the death of Ergonus. He expected to join their number then but was denied. His path would have been easier with the proper rank and authority, but the work ahead is too important for internal bickering to stand in his way.

Krueger has gathered his own army; its ranks filled with those discontented with their place in the Circle's hierarchy or drawn to the Stormlord's bold and uncompromising vision. Bringing lightning and storm, blood and battle, he promises his followers to return the Circle to its primordial roots, where the weak make way for the strong and druids are free to drink deeply of nature's unchecked power.

MOHSAR THE DESERTWALKER
CIRCLE WARLOCK

He is not a force idly woken, nor is he easily quelled. I'd sooner endure an avalanche than Mohsar's wrath.

—Baldur the Stonecleaver

MOHSAR						
SPD	STR	MAT	RAT	DEF	ARM	CMD
5	4	5	6	14	14	8

DUST HOWLER			
RNG	ROF	AOE	POW
SP 8	1	—	13

WITHERTHORN		
	POW	P+S
	6	10

FURY	8
DAMAGE	**15**
FIELD ALLOWANCE	**C**
WARBEAST POINTS	**+5**
SMALL BASE	

FEAT: DISJUNCTION

Steeped in the energy flowing through Orboros, Mohsar the Desertwalker has learned to sense and disrupt spiritual manifestations. He sunders the bond between warlock and warbeast with almost casual disregard, and he can shred the delicate connection between warcasters and their arc nodes. His power ensures those who would hurl magic against the Desertwalker must do so face-to-face.

While in Mohsar's control area enemy models cannot be used to channel spells, cannot leach fury, and cannot have fury leached from them. Disjunction lasts for one round.

MOHSAR

⊚ **Eyeless Sight**

◖ **Pathfinder**

Circular Vision – This model's front arc extends to 360˚.

Maltreatment – Once per turn during its activation this model can remove 1 fury point from a warbeast in its battlegroup that is in its control area and add 1 fury point to its own current total. The warbeast suffers d3 damage points.

DUST HOWLER

⊛ **Magical Weapon**

WITHERTHORN

⊛ **Magical Weapon**

⊘ **Reach**

Erosion – This model rolls an additional die on this weapon's damage rolls against non-living models.

SPELLS	COST	RNG	AOE	POW	UP	OFF
CREVASSE	3	8	–	12	NO	YES

If Crevasse boxes its original target, you can make a SP 6 attack using the boxed model as the attack's point of origin. Models hit suffer a POW 12 magic damage roll. Models boxed by Crevasse are removed from play.

CURSE OF SHADOWS	3	8	–	–	YES	YES

Target model/unit suffers –2 ARM and cannot make free strikes. A model can advance through an affected model if it has enough movement to move completely past its base.

MIRAGE	3	6	–	–	YES	NO

Target friendly Faction model/unit gains Apparition. (During your Control Phase, place models with Apparition anywhere completely within 2˝ of their current locations. If Mirage affects a unit, only models in formation can be placed.)

PILLAR OF SALT	2	CTRL	3	–	NO	NO

Place a 3˝ AOE anywhere completely in this model's control area where it does not touch a model's base. The AOE is an obstruction that blocks LOS and provides cover. It is a structure with ARM 18 and leaves play if it suffers 1 or more damage points. The AOE remains in play for one round.

SANDS OF FATE	2	SELF	CTRL	–	NO	NO

Remove a friendly living Faction trooper model in this model's control area from play and replace it with this model. This model cannot advance this activation after being placed by Sands of Fate.

SUNHAMMER	3	SELF	CTRL	–	YES	NO

Enemy warbeasts/warjacks that advance more than 1˝ and end their normal movement in this model's control area suffer d3 damage points.

TACTICAL TIPS

MALTREATMENT – This model can exceed its FURY in fury points as a result of Maltreatment.

CREVASSE – Because a boxed model is removed from play before being destroyed, it does not generate a soul or corpse token.

MIRAGE – Remember that troopers must be placed in formation.

Of the three omnipotents presiding over the Circle Orboros, the eldest and most enigmatic is Mohsar the Desertwalker. Other druids speak his name in hushed tones, as if invoking his title might attract his unwelcome attention. The Desertwalker believes the desert wastes of the Bloodstone Marches perfectly reflect Orboros' myriad nature. The unforgiving power of nature pervades this climate, and the desert shrugs off all feeble efforts of civilization to hold it at bay. No city can outlast the shifting dunes, and to Mohsar there is no beauty purer than the cleansing wrath of a sandstorm.

Mohsar is at first an easy man to underestimate, for his milky eyes mark him as blind. This trait hinders him little, however; his awareness of Orboros is perfect. Letting his consciousness flow into his surroundings, he takes in the entirety of the landscape around him.

Mohsar has learned to manifest the tremendous powers of his environment. The land cracks open at his command to swallow armies whole; pillars of salt erupt to block narrow passes; and impossible heat hammers down from the sky to punish beast and machine alike. Even more terrifying is that these powers seem to cost him very little, as if the greatest feats of natural magic require nothing more than walking the shifting sands.

Mohsar's loathing of humanity is legendary, and even his fellows he tolerates only when absolutely necessary. Any army he calls to battle is disposable, a force to be spent toward his ends. Despite the callousness of his approach, the allies of Orboros fear him too much to refuse his summons. Those who learn Mohsar tutored Krueger immediately gain insight into the mettle of the Stormlord's soul. Yet even then their imaginations cannot fully comprehend the cruel savagery Mohsar inflicted upon his apprentice in an effort to grind him into perfection, raze away his flaws, and elevate him bleeding and screaming to the dizzying heights of his inner potential. Mohsar is as relentless as the sun and

emanates scornful disregard as palpable as the hot wind blowing across the dunes.

Mohsar has recently involved himself once more in Circle affairs, and his reappearance has troubled more than his enemies. Perhaps his blind eyes show him the shadow of a black cloud the other omnipotents cannot see. He takes no one into his counsel, and even those who serve him can only guess at his thoughts.

MORVAHNA THE AUTUMNBLADE
CIRCLE WARLOCK

Do not mistake her sweet words for aught but naked ambition. She is as cruel as she is beautiful, and every flower that blooms at her touch exacts a price in blood.

—Baldur the Stonecleaver

MORVAHNA						
SPD	STR	MAT	RAT	DEF	ARM	CMD
6	5	6	4	15	13	9

EQUINOX		
	POW	P+S
	7	12

FURY	7
DAMAGE	14
FIELD ALLOWANCE	C
WARBEAST POINTS	+6
SMALL BASE	

FEAT: SEEDS OF DESTRUCTION

No one better understands how life is linked to death than Morvahna the Autumnblade. She has the fearsome power to spawn new life from the deaths of her foes. Each killing stroke is a sacrifice that erupts into thorny branches and blood-soaked leaves of flesh-born trees.

When a friendly Faction model destroys a living or undead enemy model with a melee attack while in Morvahna's control area this turn, center a 3″ AOE on the destroyed model and remove that model from the table. The AOE is forest terrain that remains in play for one round. Enemy models in the AOE when it is put in play are hit and suffer an unboostable POW 13 blast damage roll.

MORVAHNA

- 🖐 Pathfinder

Sacrificial Pawn [Faction warrior] – When this model is directly hit by an enemy ranged attack, you can choose to have one friendly, non-incorporeal Faction warrior model within 3″ of this model directly hit instead. That model is automatically hit and suffers all damage and effects.

EQUINOX

- ⊘ Magical Weapon
- ⊘ Reach

Harrow – An enemy model damaged by this weapon suffers Harrow for one round. Once per turn this model can transfer damage from an enemy attack to an enemy model with Harrow.

SPELLS	COST	RNG	AOE	POW	UP	OFF
ERUPTION OF LIFE	3	10	–	13	NO	YES

If this attack destroys a living or undead enemy model, center a 3″ AOE on the destroyed model before removing it from the table. The AOE is forest terrain that remains in play for one round. Enemy models in the AOE when it is put in play are hit and suffer an unboostable POW 13 blast damage roll.

HARVEST	3	SELF	CTRL	–	YES	NO

When a living or undead enemy model is destroyed in this model's control area, this model can gain 1 fury point. This model's fury point total cannot exceed its FURY as a result of Harvest.

INFLUENCE	1	10	–	–	NO	YES

Take control of target enemy non-warcaster, non-warlock warrior model. The model immediately makes one normal melee attack, then Influence expires.

REGROWTH	4	6	–	–	YES	NO

Target friendly living Faction small-based unit. During the Control Phase this model can spend 1 or more fury points. For each fury point spent, return one destroyed Grunt to the unit. It must be placed in this model's control area in formation and within 3″ of another model in its unit. The Grunt is returned with one unmarked damage box.

RESTORATION	2	6	–	–	YES	NO

Target friendly Faction model/unit gains +2 ARM. When this spell is upkept, this model heals 1 damage point for each friendly model affected by Restoration within 1″ of this model.

TACTICAL TIPS

REGROWTH – Remember, the Grunt can activate normally with its unit this turn.

RESTORATION – Morvahna is the model that heals.

Morvahna culls the living and restores the dying with equal skill. Forests spring forth at her command and tear her foes asunder as the trees draw sustenance from the last flow of life's blood. She is the Autumnblade, whose arrival portends the dark turning of the year. No druid willingly earns her enmity, and many seek her favor.

Known as a woman of great intelligence, ambition, and persuasive charm, Morvahna revels in the intrigue within the ranks of the Circle Orboros and sees her eventual ascension to omnipotent as a foregone conclusion. With a seductive smile, a caress, and a calm word she achieves more than others manage with armies or the full brunt of elemental forces.

Morvahna was inculcated in the mysteries of spring and autumn from infancy. She matured in isolation among druids of the far south on an unnamed island off the Mercir coast. Her sect knew that across the waters dragons awaited: Lord Toruk to the west and Blighterghast to the north. She has wrestled with the blight and experimented with druidic

power to try to cleanse the outer Scharde Isles of it. Her territory has shifted north and expanded over the decades; on the grounds of sacred sites others once claimed now stand forests watered with the blood of Morvahna's rivals.

Of her peers, only Krueger has dared challenge her directly, even stealing the loyalty of one of her most formidable allies—Kromac the Ravenous. The timing of this was poor, as Morvahna has been at the forefront of the Circle's battles against the Legion of Everblight. As a pragmatic woman she found help elsewhere, convincing Kaya the Moonhunter to assist her. Morvahna has endured a number of difficult setbacks against the Legion, including the battle at the Castle of the Keys and the subsequent pursuit of the Legion forces north. She holds Krueger to blame for the order's botched attempt to prevent the expansion of Everblight's power, as the Stormlord diverted critical assets from the fight with his own unrelated schemes.

Morvahna's primary flaw is her arrogance. She often underestimates others, relying on manipulation over true loyalty. She has no inclination for deeper attachments. She is willing to stand in the gateway between life and death and feels qualified to judge who should live and who will be destroyed.

GORAX
CIRCLE LIGHT WARBEAST

Our command of the gorax is a mirror of our relationship with the Wurm: any control we exert is at best temporary.
—Krueger the Stormwrath

ANIMUS	COST	RNG	AOE	POW	UP	OFF
PRIMAL	2	6	–	–	NO	NO

Target friendly living warbeast gains +2 STR and MAT for one round and automatically frenzies during your next Control Phase.

TACTICAL TIPS

PRIMAL – The warbeast frenzies even if Primal was removed via a spell, ability, or casting of new animus on the same model prior to the Control Phase.

GORAX

Pain Response – While damaged this model can charge or make power attacks without being forced.

CLAW

👊 Open Fist

GORAX						
SPD	STR	MAT	RAT	DEF	ARM	CMD
5	9	6	3	12	16	5

CLAW		
L	POW	P+S
	3	12

CLAW		
R	POW	P+S
	3	12

FURY	4
THRESHOLD	8
FIELD ALLOWANCE	U
POINT COST	4
MEDIUM BASE	

Falling somewhere between beast and man, gorax are hulking primitives with broad and massively muscular torsos that boast extremely long arms ending in oversized claws. Their jaws protrude from ugly faces and are filled with hardened fangs designed to tear the flesh and sinew that form the bulk of their carnivorous diet. Few creatures better embody the primal and uncontrollable rage of a warbeast than gorax. But even these terrible attributes pale in the face of their terrifying reaction to pain: rather than slow them down, injuries drive them to lash out with ever-increasing savagery and strength.

For centuries gorax have been captured, enslaved, and trained for battle. Warlords of the Thousand Cities era used them as front-line shock troops, flinging them into frenzied melee by the hundreds. Once the creatures' blood lust became too great to control, they were simply killed. Gorax appreciate the taste of human flesh, and some prefer it above all other fare. Their tendency to attack friend and foe alike quickly diminished their use in the wars of man, but the druids have again pulled them from their wilderness lairs to terrorize western Immoren.

Despite their fearsome appearance, gorax are smarter than animals. They have a guttural approximation of speech and can learn to follow instructions. The druids have bribed them with food and mates, for they are conditioned to accept training and do not require armament to fight effectively. The Circle taps into the primal chaos seething deep within the maddened minds of gorax and spreads that raw strength like a fever among other warbeasts—transforming untapped aggression into bestial destruction.

WOLDWATCHER
CIRCLE LIGHT WARBEAST

In the lands of Orboros, even the stones have eyes.

—Kaya the Wildborne

WOLDWATCHER						
SPD	STR	MAT	RAT	DEF	ARM	CMD
5	8	5	5	10	17	—

ELEMENTAL STRIKE			
RNG	ROF	AOE	POW
10	1	—	12

RUNE FIST	
POW	P+S
4	12
L

RUNE FIST	
POW	P+S
4	12
R

FURY	2
THRESHOLD	-
FIELD ALLOWANCE	U
POINT COST	5
MEDIUM BASE	

WOLDWATCHER

⊙ **Advance Deployment**

⊘ **Construct**

☾ **Pathfinder**

Shield Guard – Once per round, when a friendly model is directly hit by a ranged attack during your opponent's turn while within 2″ of this model, this model can become the target of the attack and be automatically hit instead. This model cannot use Shield Guard if it is incorporeal, knocked down, or stationary.

Stone Form – During its activation, this model can be forced to use Stone Form. For one round or until it advances, this model gains +4 ARM, its base DEF is reduced to 5, and it is automatically hit by melee attacks.

ELEMENTAL STRIKE

⊘ **Magical Weapon**

Fertilizer – When a living or undead model is boxed by this weapon, center a 3″ AOE on it and then remove the model from play. The AOE is a forest that remains in play for one round.

RUNE FIST

⊘ **Magical Weapon**

✊ **Open Fist**

Fertilizer – See above.

ANIMUS	COST	RNG	AOE	POW	UP	OFF
EARTH'S BLESSING	1	SELF	–	–	NO	NO

This model cannot be pushed, knocked down, or made stationary. Earth's Blessing lasts for one round.

TACTICAL TIPS

SHIELD GUARD – If this model cannot become the target of the attack for some reason, it cannot use this ability.

FERTILIZER – Because the boxed model is removed from play before being destroyed, it does not generate a soul or corpse token.

the earth can fashion them from any strong stone and other natural materials lashed together by ropes that have tasted blood. Into the stone the druids inscribe ancient runes imbuing the woldwatcher with the power of Orboros and the spark of animation. Many druids prefer these versatile elemental constructs to their larger counterparts, for they are easier to assemble and endlessly useful.

Although the ropes used to make woldwatchers are not always wound from vines watered with the blood of sacrifices as they once were, the constructs still draw great power from the essence of life. Their strong connection to the earth allows them to cause a brief but dramatic explosion in plant growth and to become nearly impervious simply by standing still.

Drawing upon the strength of stone, soil, and tree, woldwatchers defend sacred groves and screen the advancing armies of the Circle. It is impossible to doubt their power after witnessing enemies overcome by blasts of elemental energy that sunder bodies in showers of blood that feed the hungry earth. A grove of trees then erupts from this still-twitching flesh, tearing apart what remains of the victim in a plume of gore.

Rolled up into tight piles of easily overlooked stone, woldwatchers are often placed to protect key territories in the forest. When triggered by the tread of intruders, they reveal their true form and call upon the power of nature to neutralize interlopers. Blackclads who honor the ways of

WOLDWYRD
CIRCLE LIGHT WARBEAST

The unnatural powers of our enemies will be their undoing.
—Kaya the Moonhunter

ANIMUS	COST	RNG	AOE	POW	UP	OFF
ARCANE SUPPRESSION	2	SELF	–	–	NO	NO

While within 10″ of this model, enemy models must pay double fury and focus points to cast or upkeep spells. Arcane Suppression lasts for one round.

Of all the elemental constructs built by the shapers of stone, the woldwyrd is the most overtly arcane. The druids designed the woldwyrd to be a small but potent sentinel, calibrating every inch of its rune-covered surface to tap directly into the invisible lattice of ley lines surging beneath the soil. A woldwyrd floats silently above the earth, its large polished orb of pure beryl pulsing green like a wrathful eye. This glow can brighten in an instant to a blinding intensity, just before the stone unleashes a deadly beam potent enough to sear flesh, melt iron, and end lives in a blaze of emerald fire.

WOLDWYRD

- Construct
- Gunfighter
- Pathfinder

Steady – This model cannot be knocked down.

Witch Hunter – After an enemy model casts a spell within 10″ of this model, this model can immediately make a normal ranged attack targeting that model.

ARCANE STRIKE

- Magical Weapon

Purgation – Gain an additional die on attack and damage rolls with this weapon against models with an enemy upkeep spell on them.

WOLDWYRD						
SPD	STR	MAT	RAT	DEF	ARM	CMD
7	6	3	6	13	16	—

ARCANE STRIKE			
RNG	ROF	AOE	POW
10	3	–	10

FURY	3
THRESHOLD	-
FIELD ALLOWANCE	U
POINT COST	5
MEDIUM BASE	

Few enemies of the Circle have lived to tell of encounters with these unrelenting hunters, which were designed to strike down wielders of magic. It matters not if a foe lays claim to occult mastery, priestly sanctity, or arcane strength—all fall before the merciless fire of the woldwyrds. In ancient times woldwyrds hunted tradition-bound Menite priests, who burned anyone who manifested the wilding.

The expanding battles of the druids of Orboros have prompted the construction of more of these guardians. Many blackclads value them as tools of tremendous versatility against those who would dare contest the Circle for mastery of the wilderness.

SHADOWHORN SATYR
CIRCLE HEAVY WARBEAST

Call them from the mountains and let us unleash their savagery upon the enemies of Orboros.

—Krueger the Stormlord

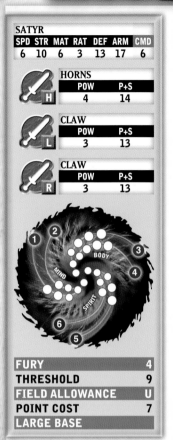

SATYR						
SPD	STR	MAT	RAT	DEF	ARM	CMD
6	10	6	3	13	17	6

HORNS (H)

	POW	P+S
	4	14

CLAW (L)

	POW	P+S
	3	13

CLAW (R)

	POW	P+S
	3	13

FURY	4
THRESHOLD	9
FIELD ALLOWANCE	U
POINT COST	7
LARGE BASE	

SATYR

Bounding Leap – Once per activation, after making a full advance but before performing an action, this model can be forced to be placed completely within 5″ of its current location. Any effects that prevent charging also prevent this model from using Bounding Leap.

Reversal – When a model misses this model with a charge or a power attack, the attacking model is knocked down.

Set Defense – A model in this model's front arc suffers –2 on charge, slam power attack, and impact attack rolls against this model.

HORNS

Hard Head – This model can add this weapon's POW to its head-butt and slam power attack damage rolls.

CLAW

👊 **Open Fist**

ANIMUS	COST	RNG	AOE	POW	UP	OFF
VIRILITY	1	6	–	–	NO	NO

Target friendly living Faction warbeast can make power attacks during its activation without being forced. A model that is power attack slammed or thrown by the affected warbeast is moved an additional +2″. Virility lasts for one turn.

The shadowhorns' love of battle is evident even in their clashes in the wild. As with other satyrs, many of these contests take place between mature males competing to mate. Though their bodies are leaner than those of some of their cousins, their nimble athleticism makes them capable of impressive feats, such as using the momentum of an attacker against it. Whereas the gnarlhorns clash head-to-head with ear-splitting impacts, the shadowhorns engage in leaping martial dances, springing off tree trunks and passing one another in blurs of motion. Foes that close with a shadowhorn are often quickly sent flying through the air, their bodies shattering against the nearest trees.

Satyrs are elusive creatures who have endured by avoiding the sight of mankind. Only recently have the druids called them forth from their remote mountain and forest lairs to join the battles abroad. Of the numerous hardy satyr breeds, some are better equipped for warfare than others. The swift and agile shadowhorns, for example, have entered the fray with particular enthusiasm. Shadowhorns possess a slenderer build than the gnarlhorns, but their energetic personalities are even more aggressive and they display a particularly savage glee when closing with the enemy.

GNARLHORN SATYR
CIRCLE HEAVY WARBEAST

If a locomotive and a charging satyr collided, only the satyr would still be standing when the dust cleared.
—Alten Ashley

ANIMUS	COST	RNG	AOE	POW	UP	OFF
BOUNDING	2	6	–	–	NO	NO

Target friendly Faction warbeast gains +2″ movement if it charges or makes a slam or trample power attack. The affected model also gains +2 on charge, slam, and trample attack rolls. Bounding lasts for one turn.

TACTICAL TIPS

BOUNDING – Modifiers to movement apply only to a model's normal movement.

FOLLOW UP – This model stops moving if it contacts another model. This model does not advance if the model slammed is destroyed by the attack.

Gnarlhorn satyrs are creatures of pure strength and unyielding force. At a dead run their massive horns are capable of ramming foes with steel-buckling power. Creatures naïve enough to prey upon satyrs inevitably receive a bone-shattering response likely to send them flying like rag dolls. Such crushing encounters also take place between males vying for mates and territory.

SATYR

Counter Slam – When an enemy model advances and ends its movement within 6″ and in the LOS of this model, this model can immediately make a slam power attack against that model. If this model makes a counter slam, it cannot make another until after your next turn. This model cannot make a counter slam while engaged.

Follow Up – When this model slams an enemy model, immediately after the slam is resolved this model can advance directly toward the slammed model up to the distance the slammed model was moved.

Grand Slam – This model can make slam power attacks without spending focus or being forced. Models slammed by this model are moved an additional 2″.

HORNS

Hard Head – This model can add this weapon's POW to its head-butt and slam power attack damage rolls.

CLAW
🖐 Open Fist

SATYR						
SPD	STR	MAT	RAT	DEF	ARM	CMD
6	11	6	3	12	18	7

HORNS	
POW	P+S
4	15

CLAW L	
POW	P+S
3	14

CLAW R	
POW	P+S
3	14

FURY	4
THRESHOLD	9
FIELD ALLOWANCE	U
POINT COST	8
LARGE BASE	

Blackclads have for centuries done much to hide these creatures from the eyes of man. Believing satyrs to be the embodiment of the hated Devourer Wurm, ignorant humans once hunted them at every opportunity. The Circle Orboros found satyrs both useful and loyal and helped preserve them from extinction.

Because satyrs will not abide mistreatment of those they protect, the Circle often takes them as personal guardians. Threatening a druid protected by a satyr first provokes the thunderous sound of hoofbeats, then the creature lowers its head and strikes with force traumatic enough to turn bones to jelly and flesh to paste.

FERAL WARPWOLF
CIRCLE HEAVY WARBEAST

They embody the essence of the Beast of All Shapes. To watch them devour our enemies is to see the hand of Orboros at work.

—Krueger the Stormwrath

WARPWOLF						
SPD	STR	MAT	RAT	DEF	ARM	CMD
6	11	7	3	14	16	7

BITE (H)
POW	P+S
3	14

CLAW (L)
POW	P+S
4	15

CLAW (R)
POW	P+S
4	15

FURY	4
THRESHOLD	9
FIELD ALLOWANCE	U
POINT COST	9
LARGE BASE	

WARPWOLF

Controlled Warping – At the beginning of this model's activation, choose one of the following warp effects. Warp effects last for one round. If this model frenzies it must choose Warp Strength at the start of its activation.

- **Protective Plates –** This model gains +2 ARM.
- **Warp Speed –** This model gains +2 SPD.
- **Warp Strength –** This model gains +2 STR.

Regeneration [d3] – This model can be forced to heal d3 damage points once per activation. This model cannot use Regeneration during an activation it runs.

CLAW
👊 Open Fist

ANIMUS	COST	RNG	AOE	POW	UP	OFF
BAYING OF CHAOS	2	SELF	*	-	NO	NO

Remove 1 fury point from each enemy warbeast in this model's command range. A warbeast can be affected by Baying of Chaos only once per turn.

Few warpwolves retain their sanity, suffering from nervousness, tension, and violent episodes even when in human form. They indulge any excuse to express their predatory nature. The Circle officially disdains the creation of new warpwolves from the unafflicted partially for this reason, but since the rise of Everblight and the unexpected feud with the trollkin, the omnipotents have turned a blind eye to the practice.

Warpwolf bodies constantly shift and warp in battle, muscles and tendons preferentially bulging to provide bursts of speed or power and bone-like spurs erupting to protect vulnerable flesh. Wounds quickly close as skin wriggles, ripples, and reforms over an injury. The bloodcurdling howls of triumphant warpwolves on the hunt is one of the most terrifying sounds in the dark wilds of western Immoren.

The embodiment of the Devourer Wurm, warpwolves were first created by a degenerate cult of Devourer worshipers seeking a closer connection to the Beast of All Shapes. They unlocked a potent mystical formula that combined the bestial essence of man with the madness associated with the shifting moons. A mortal human who ingested this elixir transformed into a hulking, bipedal, lupine monster when distressed or injured—a warpwolf, filled with the urge to slaughter and feast. Long ago a cabal within the Circle hierarchy learned the secret of the formula, and the blackclads have since used these beasts for war.

Although the initial transformation from human to warpwolf is instantaneous, after a time the beast returns to human form. The transformation cycle will occur again in times of stress and during certain lunar phases; the genetic change is irreversible. Warpwolf children possess the transformative ability of their parents.

PUREBLOOD WARPWOLF
CIRCLE HEAVY WARBEAST

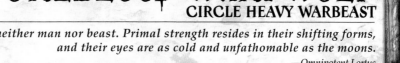

They are something neither man nor beast. Primal strength resides in their shifting forms, and their eyes are as cold and unfathomable as the moons.
—Omnipotent Lortus

ANIMUS	COST	RNG	AOE	POW	UP	OFF
WRAITHBANE	2	6	–	–	NO	NO

Target friendly Faction model's weapons gain Magical Weapon  and Blessed. Wraithbane lasts for one turn. (When making an attack with a weapon with Blessed, ignore spell effects that add to a model's ARM or DEF.)

TACTICAL TIPS

SPELL WARD – This model is shielded from friendly and enemy spells alike.

Bestial guardians boasting singular power dwell amid towering columns of rune-carved stone within the most sacred groves of Orboros. With fur as white as the light of the moon Calder, these pureblood warpwolves can call upon the supernatural essence of their blood to become as insubstantial as fog, passing through tree and wall to rend their foes. They can unleash this same primal power in a discordant howl that opens bleeding rents in flesh and can even shatter stone.

WARPWOLF

Controlled Warping – At the beginning of this model's activation, choose one of the following warp effects. Warp effects last for one round. If this model frenzies it must choose Warp Strength at the start of its activation.

- **Ghostly** – This model can advance through terrain and obstacles without penalty and can advance through obstructions if it has enough movement to move completely past them. This model cannot be targeted by free strikes.

- **Spell Ward** – This model cannot be targeted by spells.

- **Warp Strength** – This model gains +2 STR.

Leadership [Warpwolves] – While in this model's command range, friendly Warpwolf models can use Ghostly as if it were a Controlled Warping effect on their cards.

Regeneration [d3] – This model can be forced to heal d3 damage points once per activation. This model cannot use Regeneration during an activation it runs.

DEATH HOWLER
 Magical Weapon

CLAW
Open Fist

WARPWOLF						
SPD	STR	MAT	RAT	DEF	ARM	CMD
6	10	6	5	14	17	7

DEATH HOWLER			
RNG	ROF	AOE	POW
SP 10	1	—	14

CLAW	
POW	P+S
4	14

CLAW	
POW	P+S
4	14

FURY	4
THRESHOLD	10
FIELD ALLOWANCE	U
POINT COST	9
LARGE BASE	

Generations of breeding among those born as warpwolves have resulted in these great beasts, which are proudly free of the taint of man. The only indication of their humanity lies in their intelligence; though they lack the restraints of conscience, they possess cunning beyond any simple beast. Purebloods do not need a human form to speak, though their voices are rough and difficult to understand by those not accustomed to them. Senior druids have found them possessed of surprising insight and capable of adaptive tactical brilliance and bold, ruthless courage.

63

WARPWOLF STALKER
CIRCLE HEAVY WARBEAST

They are the blasphemous spawn of primordial madness, as warped in mind as they are in body.

—Vice Scrutator Vindictus

WARPWOLF						
SPD	STR	MAT	RAT	DEF	ARM	CMD
6	10	6	3	14	17	7

CLAW		
L	POW	P+S
	4	14

GREAT SWORD		
R	POW	P+S
	6	16

FURY	4
THRESHOLD	9
FIELD ALLOWANCE	U
POINT COST	10
LARGE BASE	

WARPWOLF

🌀 **Pathfinder**

Controlled Warping – At the beginning of this model's activation, choose one of the following warp effects. Warp effects last for one round. If this model frenzies it must choose Warp Strength at the start of its activation.

- **Berserk –** When this model destroys one or more models with a melee attack during its combat action, immediately after the attack is resolved it must make one additional melee attack against another model in its melee range.

- **Prowl –** This model gains Stealth 🔆 while within terrain that provides concealment, the AOE of a spell that provides concealment, or the AOE of a cloud effect.

- **Warp Strength –** This model gains +2 STR.

Regeneration [d3] – This model can be forced to heal d3 damage points once per activation. This model cannot use Regeneration during an activation it runs.

GREAT SWORD

⟳ **Reach**

CLAW

✊ **Open Fist**

ANIMUS	COST	RNG	AOE	POW	UP	OFF
LIGHTNING STRIKE	2	6	–	–	NO	NO

Target friendly model gains Sprint. Lightning Strike lasts for one turn. (At the end of its activation, if a model with Sprint destroyed one or more enemy models with melee attacks this activation it can make a full advance.)

Some arcanists of the order have speculated that those who become warpwolf stalkers were individuals touched by the shadow of the wilding. Though they lack the spark that would have enabled them to become true blackclads, their transformation gives them access to a font of primal power.

These creatures prowl the forests of Immoren and accompany the vanguard of the Circle's armies. Concealed amid the dense foliage they stalk their quarry quietly even as their rage grows and threatens to grow out of control. At the last possible moment, the stalkers leap out and slaughter their unsuspecting prey in a berserk rush of liberated frenzy.

Warpwolf stalkers are created from the same fell rites used to spawn feral warpwolves. For reasons not entirely understood, however, these creatures react differently to the transformative elixir. Though unquestionably warped by the savage power of the Devourer, stalkers retain a portion of their human intellect and are able to wield weapons even after warping into their bestial forms. With this combination of bestial instinct and human faculty, they are particularly effective weapons, if still bloodthirsty in the extreme.

The mountains and forests themselves march with us; our army rises from the very land we are sworn to protect.
—Baldur the Stonecleaver

ANIMUS	COST	RNG	AOE	POW	UP	OFF
WILD GROWTH	2	SELF	–	–	NO	NO

Center a 4" AOE on this model. The AOE is a forest that remains in play for one round.

Woldwardens are towering constructs that combine the permanence of stone and wood with the chaos of living entropy. Their solid frames are inscribed with intricate lattices of runes that glow when infused with the power of Orboros. With mighty stone fists strengthened by nature's wrath, these elemental monoliths can deliver an overwhelming onslaught of terrible blows.

A woldwarden's greatest asset is the mystical harmony it enjoys with its controlling warlock. This bond allows the woldwarden to be a vessel for the druid's arcane might, which is fueled by the power of the earth rather than the druid's own energy. A woldwarden can unleash potent magic, effectively allowing its controlling druid to attack from two places at once. More than a mere weapon, the woldwarden is

WOLDWARDEN

⊙ **Construct**

🜂 **Pathfinder**

Geomancy – Once per activation while in its controller's control area, this model can be forced to cast one of its warlock's spells with a COST of 3 or less. This model's controller is considered to have cast the spell but this model is its point of origin. When making a magic attack roll, this model uses its controller's FURY. This model cannot cast spells with a RNG of SELF or CTRL.

RUNE FIST

⊙ **Magical Weapon**

🖐 **Open Fist**

Chain Attack: Smite – If this model hits the same model with both its initial attacks with this weapon, after resolving the attacks it can immediately make one additional melee attack against that model. If the additional attack hits, the target is slammed d6" directly away from this model. The POW of the slam damage roll is equal to the STR of this model + the POW of this weapon. The POW of collateral damage is equal to the STR of this model.

WOLDWARDEN

SPD	STR	MAT	RAT	DEF	ARM	CMD
5	11	6	4	10	18	—

RUNE FIST		
L	POW	P+S
	4	15

RUNE FIST		
R	POW	P+S
	4	15

FURY	3
THRESHOLD	-
FIELD ALLOWANCE	U
POINT COST	9
LARGE BASE	

an extension of its druid's will and embodies the absolute power he wields within his territory.

Crafted from huge blocks of stone and inscribed with countless powerful sigils, a woldwarden is created from a slow process that imbues it with the will of its creator. In quiet times woldwardens guard the most sacred sites of the Circle Orboros, but in the current crisis they have been brought forth from those groves to contest directly with the Circle's enemies.

Some druids, particularly those who follow the path of earth, consider woldwardens superior to and infinitely more reliable than the wild beasts others struggle to tame. Woldwardens can charge unimpeded through any terrain and absorb tremendous punishment in battle. Their natural power allows them to cause trees and foliage to erupt around them, hindering any enemy that attempts to engage them.

WOLD GUARDIAN
CIRCLE HEAVY WARBEAST

Like the mountain it is indomitable, but within roils the destructiveness of an avalanche.

—Baldur the Stonecleaver

WOLD GUARDIAN						
SPD	STR	MAT	RAT	DEF	ARM	CMD
4	12	6	1	9	20	—

RAM FIST (L)
POW	P+S
5	17

RAM FIST (R)
POW	P+S
5	17

FURY	3
THRESHOLD	-
FIELD ALLOWANCE	U
POINT COST	9
LARGE BASE	

WOLD GUARDIAN

- Construct
- Pathfinder

Empathic Transference – A friendly Faction warlock can transfer damage to this model even if this model has a number of fury points equal to its current FURY.

Girded – This model does not suffer blast damage. Friendly models B2B with it do not suffer blast damage.

Steady – This model cannot be knocked down.

RAM FIST

- Magical Weapon

Ram – When an enemy model is hit by this weapon, it is knocked down and can be pushed 1" directly away from this model. If it is pushed, this model can immediately advance directly toward the pushed model up to the distance that model was moved.

ANIMUS	COST	RNG	AOE	POW	UP	OFF
FLESH OF CLAY	2	SELF	–	–	NO	NO

When this model is hit by a ranged attack, the attacker rolls one less damage die. Flesh of Clay lasts for one round.

spilled across the giant form's ropes, wood, and stones in order to stir it to life. The blood suffuses the guardian's body, paying the mystical price to bestow the vitality and resiliency of the living.

The lumbering guardians might take time to reach their enemies, but once within reach death is almost inevitable. Their enormous pillar-like arms can effortlessly dash apart any obstacle that dares block their path. Those unfortunate enough to be on the receiving end of their overwhelming assaults are crushed to unidentifiable pulp, leaving behind only a bloody smear upon the earth to mark the futility of opposing the will of the Circle Orboros.

Circle druids create their constructs using the same finesse and pragmatism with which they manage warbeast breeding; each construct is produced to meet a specific need of the blackclads. The enormous wold guardians fulfill two purposes: they defend their warlocks from enemy assaults and deliver crushing blows in return. Few creatures walking Caen have the courage to stand up to the might of Circle wold guardians, which are like unyielding walking walls armed with battering rams of solid stone.

Creating a wold guardian requires large quantities of stone that must be painstakingly shaped and etched with arcane runes. The rites by which the constructs are awoken to their limited consciousnesses are equally taxing. Gallons of living blood must be

MEGALITH
CIRCLE CHARACTER HEAVY WARBEAST

*Sometimes the stone speaks to the shaper. Before I carved the first rune
I knew this one would outlast me.*
—Baldur the Stonecleaver

ANIMUS	COST	RNG	AOE	POW	UP	OFF
UNDERGROWTH	2	SELF	–	–	NO	NO

While within 5″ of this model, enemy models treat open terrain as rough terrain and suffer –2 DEF. Undergrowth lasts for one round.

TACTICAL TIPS

GEOMANCY – This is limited to the spells on the warlock's card, not the animi he can cast. This model can be forced to boost attack or damage rolls.

All wolds are constructs of massive stone blocks set into a framework of wood and vine, with runes carved along their forms marking them as extensions of their druidic creators. Among them one walks apart: Baldur's masterpiece, Megalith. Its branches and vines are still alive, and below its heavy tread its roots sink deep into the ground—both to steady its motion and to drink primal energy from the earth.

MEGALITH

⊘ **Construct**

◐ **Pathfinder**

Affinity [Baldur] – If this model is in Baldur's control area at the start of Baldur's activation, Baldur automatically heals d3 damage points.

Bountiful Restoration – During your Control Phase, remove d3 damage points from this model. During your Control Phase, remove 1 damage point from friendly Woldwardens B2B with it.

Geomancy – Once per activation while in its controller's control area, this model can be forced to cast one of its warlock's spells with a COST of 3 or less. This model's controller is considered to have cast the spell but this model is its point of origin. When making a magic attack roll, this model uses its controller's FURY. This model cannot cast spells with a RNG of SELF or CTRL.

Steady – This model cannot be knocked down.

RUNE FIST

⊘ **Magical Weapon**

✊ **Open Fist**

Weight of Stone – When a model is damaged by this weapon it suffers –3 SPD and DEF for one round.

MEGALITH						
SPD	STR	MAT	RAT	DEF	ARM	CMD
5	11	7	4	10	19	—

RUNE FIST		
L	POW	P+S
	5	16

RUNE FIST		
R	POW	P+S
	5	16

FURY	4
THRESHOLD	-
FIELD ALLOWANCE	C
POINT COST	11
LARGE BASE	

Megalith's eyes glow with something like self-awareness. This stone goliath wanders where it believes itself most needed, often finding Baldur just when its master requires aid. After being damaged in battle the cracks along its stones seal themselves, vanishing into the granite as if it were living skin. By drawing on the power of Orboros, Megalith can prompt vibrant forest growth to erupt around it.

Baldur had long considered blending living wood with stone to create a construct that was as much art as engineering. He nurtured the living elements of Megalith's form while sculpting granite around them, laboring for almost a month on the final fusion. When Baldur fell in battle to the blighted arrows of the Legion of Everblight, it was Megalith that clung to the last thread of his life and began the slow process of regrowing its master bit by bit, returning the gift of creation.

The druids of the Circle Orboros can call upon an incredibly diverse fighting force in times of need, one that is vastly different than those of their enemies yet no less effective. Their martial forces are composed of low-ranking druids, numerous warrior families that have served the druids for generations, and various savage peoples throughout western Immoren with whom they have developed relationships over the millennia. These groups, although not as numerous as many of the Circle's enemies, more than make up for their smaller numbers with great skill at arms, a deep understanding of woodlore, and a fierce devotion to the druids' causes.

At the core of the Circle fighting forces are the packs of wolfskin-clad Wolves of Orboros. These toughened wilderness warriors are drawn from families in isolated villages within the wild places of western Immoren. The Wolves are greatly feared by their foes, for they are quite adept at hunting and slaying enemies of the Circle.

The Wolves have an ancient tradition of service to the druids of the Circle, and in return the druids protect and shelter their families in the remote and clannish wilderness communities. This is partly payment for services rendered, but the arrangement also affords the Circle access and influence to manipulate certain bloodlines in which the wilding is particularly strong in the hopes of producing more druids. Traditionally, the Wolves of Orboros have served the druids of the Circle out of a time-honored fealty handed down over many generations. However, in order to join the ranks of their brethren all Wolves must demonstrate skill with the group's traditional weapons and the ability to survive in the hostile wilds. In recent years the numbers required for the escalating battles of the blackclads has required also recruiting individuals of more mercenary inclinations.

The second group of warriors that serve the Circle are the Tharn, fierce barbarians clinging to a way of life that has long since otherwise vanished from the world. While the blackclads deliberately created the Wolves of Orboros as a martial organization to serve their needs, the order's alliance with the Tharn is different. The Tharn have traditionally fought for the druids because they see the blackclads as spiritual emissaries of their patron god, the Devourer Wurm. When Morvahna the Autumnblade recently released them from the dire effects of a terrible curse known as the Ten Ills, it reinforced their steadfast loyalty not only

WEAPONS OF THE CIRCLE

The forces of the Circle Orboros wield an array of distinctive weapons designed to both emulate the natural power the Circle reveres and serve as effective tools of war. The cleft-bladed spears and swords wielded by the Wolves of Orboros are examples of this design: twin-bladed spears provide incredible penetrating power as well as being emblematic of the forked tongue of a serpent, a recurring symbol of the Devourer Wurm. This symbol is seen to some degree on many Circle weapons, from the notched axes of the Tharn to the greatswords of the warpwolf stalkers.

Among the most unusual weapons seen among the warriors and druids of the Circle Orboros are the wooden voulges wielded by the blackclads. These massive, axe-like weapons are constructed from hardwood, such as oak or walnut, and then enhanced with druidic magic. The result is a weapon every bit as durable and sharp as the finest steel, yet one that retains a link to the vital power of nature that all druids wield and shape to their own designs.

to her but also to the entire Circle Orboros. Additionally, the Tharn are a savage people and the constant opportunity for bloodshed provided to them by the Circle is more than enough motivation for most to join the druids in battle.

The Tharn are supernaturally gifted warriors and can enhance their fearsome skill at arms by channeling the destructive power of the Devourer Wurm. All Tharn can effect a terrifying transformation that instills their bodies with the strength, speed, and mien of a savage predator. Only loosely organized, these warriors generally operate at a tribal level in battle, where their strength and speed adds a terrific might to any Circle fighting force they support.

Though both the Tharn and the Wolves of Orboros are called upon to fight for the Circle in times of need, neither group is privy to the greater purpose of their druidic masters.

Rather, they are given a specific task—usually involving the destruction of Circle enemies—and then set loose like hounds on the hunt. The individual bands of Tharn and Wolves of Orboros summoned may originate from far and wide across a druid's territory, and although they may fight alongside one another, the societies tend to stay within their respective communities. This gives Circle armies a very different disposition and appearance than those of their enemies; instead of facing arrayed ranks and formations, enemies of the Circle must deal with an organic collection of skilled warriors operating in smaller units, together flowing across the battlefield like a living thing.

DRUIDS OF ORBOROS
CIRCLE UNIT

To preserve natural order, we must be prepared to harness primordial forces to hold the predations of the civilized world at bay.

—Krueger the Stormwrath

LEADER & GRUNTS						
SPD	STR	MAT	RAT	DEF	ARM	CMD
6	6	5	4	14	13	9

VOULGE		
	POW	P+S
	4	10

FIELD ALLOWANCE	2
LEADER & 5 GRUNTS	7
SMALL BASE	

LEADER

◐ Pathfinder

Camouflage – This model gains an additional +2 DEF when benefiting from concealment or cover.

Magic Ability [7]

- **Counter Magic (★Action)** – While within 3″ of this model + 1″ for each other model in this unit that is in formation, enemy models cannot cast spells and friendly models cannot be targeted by enemy spells. Counter Magic lasts for one round.

- **Force Bolt (★Attack)** – Force Bolt is a RNG 10, POW 10 magic attack. An enemy model hit by this attack can be pushed d3″ directly toward or away from this model. Choose the direction before rolling the distance. On a critical hit, the enemy model is knocked down after being pushed.

- **Medicate (★Action)** – RNG 3. Target friendly Faction warbeast. If the warbeast is in range, it heals d3 damage points. A warbeast can be affected by Medicate only once per turn.

- **Summon Vortex (★Action)** – Center a 3″ AOE cloud effect on this model. Enemy models suffer –2 to attack rolls while in the AOE. Summon Vortex lasts for one round.

GRUNTS

◐ Pathfinder

Camouflage – See above.

Magic Ability [7]

- **Force Bolt (★Attack)** – See above.

- **Medicate (★Action)** – See above.

- **Summon Vortex (★Action)** – See above.

VOULGE

⊘ Magical Weapon

⊘ Reach

TACTICAL TIPS

CAMOUFLAGE – If a model ignores concealment or cover, it also ignores concealment or cover's Camouflage bonus.

MAGIC ABILITY – Performing a Magic Ability special action or special attack counts as casting a spell.

unnerve even the most veteran soldiers. With the wilding fresh in their blood, they gather to channel enormous natural power over the earth. The greatest among them can make the ground itself betray the enemy and swallow them whole.

Druids wield mighty voulges, but their true power lies in their mastery of primal forces. Wreathed in storm, they confound enemies with wind and mist and draw upon the chaotic energies of Orboros to disrupt and unravel magic formulae wrought by arcanists, warlocks, or priests.

Orboros druids seldom fight in the open. Dense forests part to facilitate their advance and then close to shroud them in protective cover. They prefer to keep to the trees, move through marshy swamps, or attack from the advantage of cliffs. Though sending precious druids into battle is a risk, the Circle believes they will be strengthened through conflict as the worthy rise to power and the weak are culled.

Known mainly as "blackclads" to outsiders, druids are discussed in whispers. They are seen as heralds of doom, dark cultists, and reminders of a time when mankind feared the wilderness. They are known to invoke brutal reprisal on any who interfere with their plans. Seeing multiple druids emerge from the mist of a dark forest is often enough to

DRUID OF ORBOROS OVERSEER
CIRCLE UNIT ATTACHMENT

That you intruded here in ignorance matters not. You cannot depart. Every action has consequences. You may have a moment to pray to your god.
—Overseer Miredor, Mistress of a Hundred Talons

TACTICAL TIPS

Camouflage – If a model ignores concealment or cover, it also ignores concealment or cover's Camouflage bonus.

Magic Ability – Performing a Magic Ability special action or special attack counts as casting a spell.

The Devouring – Include this model when counting models for the damage bonus.

Overseers occupy a vital tier in the hierarchy of the Circle Orboros, not yet recognized as potents but possessing more impressive abilities than the inexperienced warders. An overseer must learn not only to apply his strength to further the goals of the Circle but also to lead others effectively. He might not always understand how his mission fits into higher plans, but he knows the consequences for failure become increasingly dire.

Potents task overseers to watch specific territories and regulate the lesser druids operating within them. They must travel between sacred sites and protect them from interlopers who would defile them, calling on their subordinates and nearby Wolves of Orboros to present a show of force. An overseer moved to wrath is like the

Attachment [Druids of Orboros] – This attachment can be added to a Druids of Orboros unit.

OVERSEER

 Officer

Pathfinder

Beast Master – This model can force friendly Faction warbeasts in its command range as if it were their controlling warlock.

Camouflage – This model gains an additional +2 DEF when benefiting from concealment or cover.

Magic Ability [8]

- **Elemental Protection (★Action)** – Models in its unit gain Immunity: Cold, Immunity: Electricity, and Immunity: Fire for one round.

- **Medicate (★Action)** – RNG 3. Target friendly Faction warbeast. If the warbeast is in range, it heals d3 damage points. A warbeast can be affected by Medicate only once per turn.

- **Summon Vortex (★Action)** – Center a 3″ AOE cloud effect on this model. Enemy models suffer –2 to attack rolls while in the AOE. Summon Vortex lasts for one round.

- **The Devouring (★Attack)** – The Devouring is a RNG 10, AOE 4, POW 8 magic attack. Add 1 to the POW of the attack for each model in this unit.

Tactics: Advance Deployment – Models in this unit gain Advance Deployment.

VOULGE

Magical Weapon

Reach

OVERSEER						
SPD	STR	MAT	RAT	DEF	ARM	CMD
6	6	6	4	14	13	9

VOULGE	
POW	P+S
4	10

DAMAGE	5
FIELD ALLOWANCE	1
POINT COST	2
SMALL BASE	

darkening sky before a thunderstorm or the approaching roar of a torrential flood.

Druids at this level have experienced all the essential paths of Orboros. Tapping into these abilities provides a heady rush and the first hint of what a druid can eventually become. The earth opens at their call, wind becomes a sharp-edged weapon unleashed at the wave of a hand, wild beasts answer their unspoken summons, and they can draw upon the surrounding life force to seal the most grievous wounds. Even the ravages of the elements cannot harm them.

DRUID STONEWARD & WOLDSTALKERS
CIRCLE UNIT

They think us too few to raise armies, yet our reserves are as boundless as the sticks and stones of the forest.

—Stoneward Nalosar

STONEWARD

SPD	STR	MAT	RAT	DEF	ARM	CMD
6	6	6	4	14	13	9

VOULGE

POW	P+S
4	10

WOLDSTALKER GRUNT

SPD	STR	MAT	RAT	DEF	ARM	CMD
6	4	0	6	12	15	4

ARCANE STRIKE

RNG	ROF	AOE	POW
10	1	—	12

FIELD ALLOWANCE	2
LEADER & 5 GRUNTS	5
SMALL BASE	

STONEWARD

⚜ Officer

🌙 Pathfinder

Magic Ability

- **Concentrated Fire (★Action)** – This activation models in this unit gain a +1 cumulative bonus to ranged damage rolls for each other model in this unit that has hit an enemy model with a ranged attack this activation.

- **Zephyr (★Action)** – Models in this unit that are in formation can immediately advance up to 3″. They cannot be targeted by free strikes during this movement.

Self-Sacrifice – If this model is disabled by an enemy attack, you can choose a non-disabled model in this unit within 3″ of this model to be destroyed. If another model is destroyed as a result of Self-Sacrifice, this model heals 1 damage point.

Stone Heart – This model never flees and automatically passes command checks.

WOLDSTALKER GRUNT

⊘ Construct

🌙 Pathfinder

VOULGE

⊘ Magical Weapon

⊘ Reach

ARCANE STRIKE

⊘ Magical Weapon

Adapting to the pace of the escalating wars, the druids have turned their craft to animating even greater quantities of inert materials to create legions made of earth and stone. Once used to hunt those who despoiled places of significance to the Circle Orboros, woldstalkers are now appearing in ever greater numbers. The stonewards who craft these fast and efficient killers also lead their creations to battle.

Each woldstalker is an implement of a stoneward's will, guided by his mental commands and protected by his druidic enchantments. The blackclads steer their creations' movements and choose the targets of their searing attacks. Through his constructs, a single blackclad magnifies his power fivefold. A particular sort of discipline and concentration is required to direct multiple stalkers operating simultaneously with loose independence. This is a practiced skill for the stonewards, whose guidance lingers even after their death: a woldstalker will continue to follow its druid's last impulses, hunting its prey with inhuman perseverance.

Though woldstalkers are simple in form and function, being essentially floating conduits of concentrated energy, the collective firepower they can unleash is formidable. Each woldstalker trembles violently as glowing energy flows up its wooden frame, to be focused into a small crystal orb that unleashes a devastating blast.

72

REEVE OF ORBOROS CHIEFTAIN & STANDARD
CIRCLE UNIT ATTACHMENT

The true marksman has killed two men before putting his finger to the trigger: the one beneath his aim and the one he has marked as his next victim.
—Reeves Chieftain Tyn Relthus

Hunters without compare, the greatest chieftains of the Reeves of Orboros are among the deadliest marksmen to be found in all of western Immoren. The Reeves worship aspects of the Devourer that embody their ideals and revere the wolf as their patron totem for its sharp eyes and speed. Chieftains are joined in battle by a standard bearing a personal embodiment of this totemic ideal, often including the pelt of the greatest wolf hunted by their own hand in a ritual ceremony. They bind their tribesmen to them with vows of blood, each company more warrior cult than regiment of soldiers.

Following the silent gestures of their commanding chieftain, reeves hunt and kill with the single-mindedness of a pack of predatory beasts. The hunters move effortlessly through even the heaviest brush, taking aim at their targets in perfect harmony and firing with a coordinated discipline that would impress the most punctilious drill sergeant. They reposition after eliminating their targets, each of them reflexively moving to clear lanes of fire for their brothers. With vows of death for those who would oppose the Circle Orboros, the reeves let loose a rain of bolts upon their enemies before vanishing back into the trackless wilderness they call home.

Attachment [Reeves of Orboros] - This attachment can be added to a Reeves of Orboros unit.

CHIEFTAIN

⊘ **Combined Ranged Attack**

⦿ **Officer**

☾ **Pathfinder**

Granted: Swift Hunter – While this model is in play, models in this unit gain Swift Hunter. (When a model with Swift Hunter destroys an enemy model with a normal ranged attack, immediately after the attack is resolved it can advance up to 2".)

Hunter – This model ignores forests, concealment, and cover when determining LOS or making a ranged attack.

Snap Fire – When this model destroys one or more enemy models with a ranged attack during its combat action, immediately after that attack is resolved this model can make one normal ranged attack. Attacks gained from Snap Fire do not count against a weapon's ROF and cannot generate additional attacks from Snap Fire.

Tactics: Ranked Attacks – Models in this unit gain Ranked Attacks. (Friendly Faction models can ignore models with Ranked Attacks when determining LOS.)

STANDARD BEARER

☾ **Pathfinder**

⚑ **Standard Bearer**

CHIEFTAIN

SPD	STR	MAT	RAT	DEF	ARM	CMD
6	5	6	6	13	13	9

DOUBLE CROSSBOW
RNG	ROF	AOE	POW
12	1	–	10

BATTLE BLADE
POW	P+S
3	8

STANDARD BEARER

SPD	STR	MAT	RAT	DEF	ARM	CMD
6	5	5	5	13	13	8

CHIEFTAIN'S DAMAGE	5
FIELD ALLOWANCE	1
POINT COST	2
SMALL BASE	

THARN BLOODTRACKERS
CIRCLE UNIT

Once the hunt is called there is no escape. There is no trail we cannot follow. We are the serpent in the grass, the falcon that strikes unseen from on high.

—Ksana Stagheart

LEADER & GRUNTS

SPD	STR	MAT	RAT	DEF	ARM	CMD
7	6	6	6	14	11	8

THROWN JAVELIN

RNG	ROF	AOE	POW
7	1	—	3

FIGHTING CLAW

POW	P+S
3	9

FIELD ALLOWANCE	1
LEADER & 5 GRUNTS	5
LEADER & 9 GRUNTS	8
SMALL BASE	

LEADER & GRUNTS

▶ **Advance Deployment**

🌙 **Pathfinder**

⚗ **Stealth**

Prey – After deployment but before the first player's turn, choose an enemy model/unit to be this model/unit's prey. This model gains +2 to attack and damage rolls against its prey. When this model begins its activation within 10″ of its prey, it gains +2″ movement that activation. When the prey is destroyed or removed from play, choose another model/unit to be the prey.

THROWN JAVELIN

🎵 **Weapon Master**

Thrown – Add this model's STR to the POW of this ranged attack.

TACTICAL TIPS

PREY – Modifiers to movement apply only to a model's normal movement. Choose one model/unit to be this unit's prey.

Few have ever seen a bloodtracker clearly, and those who have say they draw shadows about them like cloaks. Though magical camouflage is an exaggeration, bloodtrackers do possess a near-supernatural ability to blend into their environment and move through even the densest underbrush with startling alacrity.

Among the Tharn it is not only the men who heed the call of the Devourer; their women are equally bloodthirsty and savage. Bloodtrackers are a remnant of ancient ways—a people of a darker time—and their choice of arms reflects this. They prefer to pierce foes from a distance with weighted javelins, but they also wield clawed bucklers to eviscerate those who close with them in melee. Bloodtrackers rarely allow their foes to get so close, however. Their lean forms are instead barely seen shadows darting through the umbral underbrush, hurling javelins with terrifying accuracy into vulnerable flanks in the shifting chaos of battle.

Those who have faced bloodtrackers fear the frenetic savagery with which these women conduct their attacks. Though they do not adopt the hulking forms of the ravagers, bloodtrackers do call upon the Devourer Wurm to imbue them with the essence of animals that strike with lightning swiftness. Their hypersensitive awareness is enhanced well beyond human limits, and they slice enemies to ribbons with savage relentlessness. Once they have chosen a target for their hunt, they will seek its destruction to the exclusion of all other concerns before selecting new prey.

She reads prophecy in the blood of our enemies and carves a destiny from their flesh.
—Kromac the Ravenous

TACTICAL TIPS

PREY – Modifiers to movement apply only to a model's normal movement. Choose one model/unit to be this unit's prey.

TACTICS: QUICK WORK – A model can make this ranged attack only if it is no longer engaged after destroying the enemy model.

Among the most renowned Tharn warriors of the modern age, Nuala is a barbarous myth come to life. Numerous *tuaths* pay homage to their savage queen, counting themselves fortunate to follow her on the warpath. Though she takes vicious pleasure in leading the bloody slaughter of her enemies, she has noble aims. Nuala would see her people restored to the grand age of the Molgur, when the cities of mankind trembled at the might of the Devourer Wurm's chosen. By careful alliances and bold strikes against her nearest enemies Nuala's tribes have prospered and increased while others have withered or been left decimated by the wars of the druids.

Nuala is as pleased to prey upon remote villages and communities as she is to battle the armies that oppose the Tharn and their Circle allies. With the finest of the bloodtrackers at her side, she begins hunting her chosen prey. She and her followers descend upon their victims in a shower of piercing javelins and lethal blows, the screams of

Attachment [Tharn Bloodtracker] – This attachment can be added to a Tharn Bloodtracker unit.

NUALA

◗ **Advance Deployment**

⌃ **Officer**

⤶ **Pathfinder**

⬗ **Stealth**

Granted: Reform – While this model is in play, after all models in its unit have completed their actions, each can advance up to 3".

Prey – After deployment but before the first player's turn, choose an enemy model/unit to be this model/unit's prey. This model gains +2 to attack and damage rolls against its prey. When this model begins its activation within 10" of its prey, it gains +2" movement that activation. When the prey is destroyed or removed from play, choose another model/unit to be the prey.

Tactics: Quick Work – Models in this unit gain Quick Work. (When a model with Quick Work destroys one or more enemy models with a melee attack during its combat action, immediately after the attack is resolved it can make one normal ranged attack. Attacks gained from Quick Work do not count against a weapon's ROF.)

THROWN JAVELIN

⬗ **Weapon Master**

Thrown – Add this model's STR to the POW of this ranged attack.

NUALA						
SPD	STR	MAT	RAT	DEF	ARM	CMD
7	6	8	7	14	11	9

THROWN JAVELIN			
RNG	ROF	AOE	POW
7	1	—	3

FIGHTING CLAW	
POW	P+S
3	9

DAMAGE	5
FIELD ALLOWANCE	C
POINT COST	2
SMALL BASE	

the dying enflaming their desire for murder. Each death is committed to the Beast of All Shapes, who looks with favor upon the feasts Nuala offers in its name and grants its protection to the tribes who bow to her.

THARN BLOODWEAVERS
CIRCLE UNIT

Fresh blood pumped by a frantic heart carries a magic of its own.
With each cut we claim that power for our own.

—Kyrie Scarmaker, priestess of the Devourer Wurm

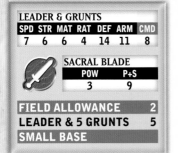

LEADER & GRUNTS						
SPD	STR	MAT	RAT	DEF	ARM	CMD
7	6	6	4	14	11	8

SACRAL BLADE		
	POW	P+S
	3	9

FIELD ALLOWANCE	2
LEADER & 5 GRUNTS	5
SMALL BASE	

LEADER & GRUNTS

(icon) Pathfinder

(icon) Stealth

Gang – When making a melee attack targeting an enemy model in melee range of another model in this unit, this model gains +2 to melee attack and melee damage rolls.

SACRAL BLADE

(icon) Magical Weapon

Bloodletting – When this model makes an attack with this weapon during its activation, choose one of the following abilities:

- **Blood Burst** – When this attack boxes a living enemy model, center a 5″ AOE on the boxed model, then remove the model from play. Enemy models in the AOE are hit and suffer a blast damage roll with a POW equal to the boxed model's STR.

- **Blood Spiller** – Gain an additional damage die against a living model.

- **Dispel** – When this weapon hits a model/unit, upkeep spells on that model/unit immediately expire.

TACTICAL TIPS

BLOOD BURST – Because the boxed model is removed from play before being destroyed, it does not generate a soul or corpse token.

DISPEL – Because they expire immediately, upkeep spells that had an effect when the model was hit or damaged will have no effect.

Tharn women who practice the rites of the bloodweavers are true masters of bloodletting. Their devotion to the Devourer Wurm is absolute, each kill a sacrifice performed with the visceral immediacy of sacral blades wielded in their own crimsoned hands.

Bloodweavers conduct ritual hunts according to the celestial conjunctions of the Eye of the Wurm, drenching themselves in the blood of the slain while singing praises to the Devourer. The holy specifics of these rites are of little consolation to their victims but involve offerings that correspond to the stars. Rarer celestial events merit greater offerings of blood and flesh and sometimes bring together larger gatherings of individual sisterhoods. Members of each tight-knit cabal have learned to fight side-by-side with smooth, practiced movements, relying solely on nonverbal cues for coordination. The silence with which they kill is followed by the chilling sound of their ecstatic chanting.

Civilized humans might dismiss the existence of these Tharn witches as superstition were it not for the gruesome remains that mark their passage. Witnessing them in battle can drive pious Menites to madness. Bloodweavers close in for the kill cloaked in animated shadows that obscure their movements. As the blades taste flesh, primal power causes the victim to erupt with sickening force, unleashing fragments of bone and gouts of blood in a torrent of boiling gore.

THARN WOLF RIDERS
CIRCLE LIGHT CAVALRY UNIT

By the time I pulled the trigger she was past me. Sarge took a javelin in the throat,
and she circled for another throw. I ran. Morrow help me, I ran screaming.
—Corporal Ian Rhoe, 95th Trencher Company

TACTICAL TIPS

ASSAULT (ORDER) – The assaulting model ignores the target in melee penalty even if is not in melee range of its charge target after moving.

PREY – Modifiers to movement apply only to a model's normal movement. Choose one model/unit to be this unit's prey.

Nothing is more terrifying than a group of Tharn on the hunt. Bloodtrackers strike their prey from the flanks and evade bullets with preternatural reflexes. Ravagers cleave enemies with axes before tearing out and feasting on their hearts. Then an eerie chorus of howls arises from all sides, and the hulking, shadowy forms of duskwolves carrying bloodtrackers emerge from the forest. Moving so quickly that enemies cannot brace for their attack, the wolves dart past and behind defenders as their bloodtracker riders hurl javelin after javelin. Duskwolves pull down their prey, bite clean through tendons and muscles, and leave enemies bleeding out their last before springing away behind the shelter of nearby trees. Soon nothing remains on the field but meat for crows.

No mere hunters of scent and blood, bloodtrackers perform fearsome rites in the name of the Devourer. Their connection to the Wurm's predator spirit allows them to form a strong

LEADER & GRUNTS
Pathfinder

Assault (Order) – Affected models must charge or run. As part of a charge, after moving but before making its charge attack, an affected model can make one ranged attack targeting the model charged unless they were in melee with each other at the start of the affected model's activation. Models that received this order cannot make combined ranged attacks this activation. When resolving an Assault ranged attack, the attacking model does not suffer the target in melee penalty. If the target is not in melee range after moving, the affected model must still make the ranged attack before its activation ends.

Hunter – This model ignores forests, concealment, and cover when determining LOS or making a ranged attack.

Prey – After deployment but before the first player's turn, choose an enemy model/unit to be this model/unit's prey. This model gains +2 to attack and damage rolls against its prey. When this model begins its activation within 10″ of its prey, it gains +2″ movement that activation. When the prey is destroyed or removed from play, choose another model/unit to be the prey.

THROWN JAVELIN
Weapon Master

Luck – This model can reroll missed attack rolls with this weapon. Each attack roll can be rerolled only once as a result of Luck.

Thrown – Add this model's STR to the POW of this ranged attack.

LEADER & GRUNTS						
SPD	STR	MAT	RAT	DEF	ARM	CMD
9	6	6	6	15	14	8

THROWN JAVELIN			
RNG	ROF	AOE	POW
7	1	—	3

JAVELIN	
POW	P+S
3	9

MOUNT
POW
12

DAMAGE	5 EA
FIELD ALLOWANCE	1
LEADER & 2 GRUNTS	6
LEADER & 4 GRUNTS	10
LARGE BASE	

bond with their chosen duskwolves, and together they become a singularly deadly hunting group. Death follows wherever they stalk, whether from silently hurled javelins or the crushing bite of a horse-sized wolf tearing out an enemy's throat.

THARN RAVAGERS
CIRCLE UNIT

They yet revel in the old ways, feasting on the hearts of the fallen and quenching their thirst in warm blood.

—Krueger the Stormwrath

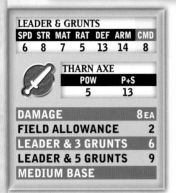

LEADER & GRUNTS						
SPD	STR	MAT	RAT	DEF	ARM	CMD
6	8	7	5	13	14	8

THARN AXE		
	POW	P+S
	5	13

DAMAGE	8 EA
FIELD ALLOWANCE	2
LEADER & 3 GRUNTS	6
LEADER & 5 GRUNTS	9
MEDIUM BASE	

LEADER & GRUNTS

✠ **Fearless**

☾ **Pathfinder**

Heart Eater – This model gains a corpse token each time it destroys a living enemy model with a melee attack. This model can have up to three corpse tokens at a time. It can spend corpse tokens during its activation to boost an attack or damage roll or to make an additional melee attack at one token per boost or additional attack.

Treewalker – This model ignores forests when determining LOS. While in a forest, this model gains +2 DEF against melee attack rolls and can advance through obstructions and other models if it has enough movement to move completely past them.

THARN AXE

⟳ **Reach**

Powerful Charge – This model gains +2 to charge attack rolls with this weapon.

Cygnar, while the rest suffered under a withering curse that decimated their numbers. Decades ago the leaders of the Circle Orboros secretly unraveled this curse and restored the Tharn's numbers, and they have once again grown strong. This renaissance, led by Morvahna the Autumnblade, has engendered the absolute loyalty of the Tharn, who are now eager to repay their debt.

The druids have encouraged the ravagers to come forth, led by their beast lords, to provide much-needed strength and ferocity to the battles being waged by the Circle Orboros. Whereas few of their other allies are eager to engage in such brutal carnage, Tharn ravagers enthusiastically charge from the forest gloom to hack apart foes with their long-handled axes. The trail of mutilated bodies they leave behind is a ghastly reminder of the dark age when civilized humans embraced the Menite priest-kings to save them from these savage tribes.

The Tharn have always been able to channel the savage power of the Devourer Wurm. In times of peace, their villages are indistinguishable from those of now largely extinct northern Khadoran barbarian tribes. In times of war, however, their populations begin to boil with bestial metamorphosis. Bellowing a call to the Wurm sends their ravagers into an unbridled frenzy of physical transformation: muscle mass expands and thickens, skin hardens, and teeth elongate into terrible fangs. Their senses become as keen as the beasts they revere, and they fall into a state of insatiable hunger. Legends of inhuman deprivation among the ravagers are true; they gleefully tear out and eat the hearts of their prey, eyes aglow with berserk madness. These acts of frenzied feasting add an element of terror to their grievous attacks.

Just three centuries ago, the Tharn numbered among the largest barbarian tribes; tens of thousands called the northern Thornwood home. Most were slaughtered as part of a political gambit by a Khadoran queen against

THARN RAVAGER CHIEFTAIN
CIRCLE UNIT ATTACHMENT

The Tharn follow their chieftains as blood follows blood: inexorably and without question.
—Lynus Wesselbaum

Becoming a chieftain among the Tharn requires far more than simply being born into a prestigious line. A chieftain must also be a great and bloody warrior and gain the absolute respect of his warriors. In addition to raw battle prowess, the Tharn also admire canny leaders who bring them prosperity. Though the Tharn live to fight without question and revel in the gifts bestowed upon them through their unique relationship with the Devourer Wurm, mindless slaughtering is not the only criterion for a revered *tuath* king. Great wisdom is also essential, for without the guiding hand of their chieftains the Tharn would never be able to gather in large numbers or form such a formidable fighting arm of the Circle Orboros.

By the time a Tharn has earned the right to be called chieftain he has led war parties and killed rivals beyond counting. Adorned with grisly trophies of his victories, the chieftain is an image out of the nightmares of civilized

Attachment [Tharn Ravagers] – This attachment can be added to a Tharn Ravagers unit.

CHIEFTAIN

✪ Fearless

⊛ Officer

☽ Pathfinder

Heart Eater – This model gains a corpse token each time it destroys a living enemy model with a melee attack. This model can have up to three corpse tokens at a time. It can spend corpse tokens during its activation to boost an attack or damage roll or to make an additional melee attack at one token per boost or additional attack.

Granted: Brutal Charge – While this model is in play, the melee weapons of models in its unit gain Brutal Charge. (A model gains +2 to charge attack damage rolls when attacking with a weapon with Brutal Charge.)

Tactics: Advance Deployment – Models in this unit gain Advance Deployment ▶.

Treewalker – This model ignores forests when determining LOS. While in a forest, this model gains +2 DEF against melee attack rolls and can advance through obstructions and other models if it has enough movement to move completely past them.

THARN AXE

⊘ Reach

Powerful Charge – This model gains +2 to charge attack rolls with this weapon.

CHIEFTAIN						
SPD	STR	MAT	RAT	DEF	ARM	CMD
6	8	8	5	13	14	9

THARN AXE		
	POW	P+S
	5	13

DAMAGE	8
FIELD ALLOWANCE	1
POINT COST	2
MEDIUM BASE	

men, the wooden haft of his well-worn axe turned black by the blood of a lifetime's killing. He is attended at all times by the greatest warriors of his tuath; indeed, to serve in a chieftain's personal guard is a great honor and reward for any Tharn. Those who fight by his side are guaranteed endless opportunities to slake their bloodthirsty urges upon the hearts of many enemies.

Each chieftain knows he leads only so long as he maintains the respect of his tribe; thus, he seeks out the heart of battle so his axe might cut a swath worthy of his name. Inspired to try to match their chieftain, his guard commits acts of violence incredible even by the bloody standards of the Tharn. Charging forward at the leading edge of every battle, a chieftain and his ravagers strive to be the first to clash with their enemies, vying for the honor of drawing first blood in the name of their tuath and their hungry god.

THARN RAVAGER SHAMAN
CIRCLE WEAPON ATTACHMENT

The Devourer's wrath splits the sky.

—Lorkash the Unrepentant, Tharn ravager shaman

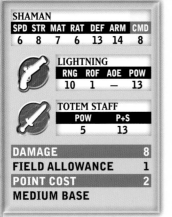

SHAMAN						
SPD	STR	MAT	RAT	DEF	ARM	CMD
6	8	7	6	13	14	8

LIGHTNING			
RNG	ROF	AOE	POW
10	1	—	13

TOTEM STAFF	
POW	P+S
5	13

DAMAGE	8
FIELD ALLOWANCE	1
POINT COST	2
MEDIUM BASE	

Attachment [Tharn Ravagers] – This attachment can be added to a Tharn Ravagers unit.

SHAMAN

⊕ **Fearless**

◐ **Pathfinder**

Assault – As part of a charge, after moving but before making its charge attack, this model can make one ranged attack targeting the model charged unless they were in melee with each other at the start of this model's activation. When resolving an Assault ranged attack, the attacking model does not suffer the target in melee penalty. If the target is not in melee range after moving, this model can make the Assault ranged attack before its activation ends.

Heart Eater – This model gains a corpse token each time it destroys a living enemy model with a melee attack. This model can have up to three corpse tokens at a time. It can spend corpse tokens during its activation to boost an attack or damage roll or to make an additional melee attack at one token per boost or additional attack.

Treewalker – This model ignores forests when determining LOS. While in a forest, this model gains +2 DEF against melee attack rolls and can advance through obstructions and other models if it has enough movement to move completely past them.

LIGHTNING

⚡ **Damage Type: Electricity**

⊗ **Magical Weapon**

Electro Leap – When a model is hit with this weapon, you can have lightning arc to the nearest model within 4″ of the model hit, ignoring the attacking model. The model the lightning arcs to suffers an unboostable POW 10 electrical damage roll ⚡.

TOTEM STAFF

⊗ **Magical Weapon**

⊘ **Reach**

Powerful Charge – This model gains +2 to charge attack rolls with this weapon.

TACTICAL TIPS

ASSAULT – The assaulting model ignores the target in melee penalty even if is not in melee range of its charge target after moving.

ELECTRO LEAP – The lightning will still arc to a model with Immunity: Electricity; it just cannot damage that model. Damage from Electro Leap is not considered to have been caused by a hit or by a melee or ranged attack.

around blazing bonfires while conducting unspeakable feast rites praising the Beast of All Shapes. Their shamans, older but no less brutal spiritual leaders, direct these revels. They continually urge on their barbaric kin, who have forsaken their human heritage to partake in ever-greater acts of carnage.

Each shaman is a dread priest of the Devourer Wurm able to call down the primal energies of scouring lighting. The devastating powers of the storm are the shaman's to command, the charred corpses of his victims littering the ground as his fellow Tharn tear into the enemy ranks.

Many often incorrectly accuse the druids of the Circle Orboros of worshipping the Devourer Wurm, when it is the Tharn who actually embody every wild story and horrific rumor associated with that ancient god. These savage terrors are accompanied by their shamans as they hunt and consume the flesh of men. They raze towns and villages, slaughter the innocent, and cavort in dark forests, chanting

WARPBORN SKINWALKERS
CIRCLE UNIT

We had no need to train the perfect warriors; we simply bred them.
—*Morvahna the Autumnblade*

Some human bloodlines are carefully nurtured by the blackclads with the same care applied to the husbandry of beasts. In the deepest wilds, the druids oversee the remote villages that shelter the Wolves of Orboros. Outsiders who stumble upon these isolated communities may initially find themselves welcomed by the people they take to be simple rustic folk. But that impression is shattered by nightfall when certain warriors of the villages begin to howl. Their skin warps and they hunt down the interlopers like prize game.

The druids of the Circle carefully choose some among the finest hunters and trackers of each generation to become part of a special breed. In distinct rituals derived from those that transform men into the savage warpwolves, the wolfborn skinwalkers commit themselves wholly to the Circle Orboros. As the agonizing ritual takes hold, their flesh distends and snouts burst forth from their faces, their skin grows hirsute, and their muscles gain strength. Their senses are also heightened, and they become near-perfect hunters. Stronger than any human, they wield their massive pole axes with enthusiastic brutality until the battle ends and they resume their mundane forms.

LEADER & GRUNTS

- Combined Melee Attack
- Fearless
- Pathfinder
- Terror

Relentless Advance – When a model in this unit is damaged by an enemy attack, models in this unit gain +2 SPD for one round.

Unyielding – While engaging an enemy model, this model gains +2 ARM.

POLE AXE

- Reach

LEADER & GRUNTS

SPD	STR	MAT	RAT	DEF	ARM	CMD
5	8	6	3	12	16	9

POLE AXE

POW	P+S
5	13

DAMAGE	8 EA
FIELD ALLOWANCE	2
LEADER & 2 GRUNTS	5
LEADER & 4 GRUNTS	8
MEDIUM BASE	

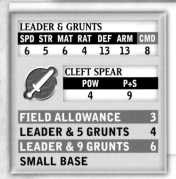

WOLVES OF ORBOROS
CIRCLE UNIT

Be wary of the people of the deep woods. Some honor ancient pacts with strange masters, and they brook no interference or questions.

—Professor Viktor Pendrake

LEADER & GRUNTS						
SPD	STR	MAT	RAT	DEF	ARM	CMD
6	5	6	4	13	13	8

CLEFT SPEAR		
	POW	P+S
	4	9

FIELD ALLOWANCE	3
LEADER & 5 GRUNTS	4
LEADER & 9 GRUNTS	6
SMALL BASE	

LEADER & GRUNTS
⚔ Combined Melee Attack
🐾 Pathfinder

CLEFT SPEAR
⚔ Reach

Powerful Charge – This model gains +2 to charge attack rolls with this weapon.

There have always been those willing to offer strength of arms to the wilderness prophets, and the Circle has used such men and women to guard their territories and serve as agents in towns and villages on the wilderness fringes. Families in the dark forests and isolated hills have passed this tradition to their sons and daughters, rugged folk initiated into a secret cabal that furthers the interests of the druids. They are the Wolves of Orboros—hunting packs marching against the enemies of whichever druidic order they promise to serve.

In exchange for this fealty, the druids vow to watch over their lands and families—a significant gesture in the brutal regions beyond civilization. Druids select these family lines because a greater than average number of their children undergo the wilding. The Circle shelters and protects such families as a precious commodity.

Each Wolf trains to master the cleft-bladed spear, a powerful piercing weapon designed to punch through thick hides and armor. Wolves of Orboros must prove their skill with this weapon and demonstrate the ability to survive in the wilds in order to pass the initiation ritual and earn the wolf pelt that marks them as a brother or sister.

With the pressure of recent battles, the Circle has bolstered the numbers of Wolves with recruits lured by offers of coin and other valuables, who serve more as mercenaries than dedicated defenders. These hardy and grim warriors must still possess pragmatic survival skills and a willingness to obey. Some cannot explain why they continue to serve after their contracts have ended, only that it feels right to do so. Coercing or intimidating men into the brotherhood is not unheard of, but the Circle knows such behavior breeds problematic resentment, so they prefer voluntary recruits. The lifestyle of the Wolves of Orboros has an undeniable appeal to those who live on the fringes of society and who hunger to belong to some greater cause.

WOLVES OF ORBOROS CHIEFTAIN & STANDARD
CIRCLE UNIT ATTACHMENT

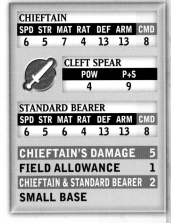

There is no escape from our hunt. Those who flee us will hear our howls the moment before death's darkness devours them.
—Master of the Hunt

TACTICAL TIPS

Officer - Because the Chieftain is an Officer, when it is destroyed it does not replace a grunt in its unit. Instead the unit leader becomes the new unit commander.

Expanding war across western Immoren has forced the Wolves to recruit many woodsmen and mercenaries into their ranks, but the core of their identity remains an ancient and primal brotherhood. Heirs to the oldest rituals and ceremonies, these warriors endure training and customs inextricably connected to the worship of the Devourer Wurm. They represent this patron of all predation with the wolf, the great pack hunter totem they revere and emulate. Only the most grizzled and scarred masters of the hunt are entrusted to lead true believers into the Wild Hunt. Any engaged in this most sacred of blood rites can be recognized by the accompanying totem that represents their vow to take no rest. They track their enemies to the ends of the earth and slaughter them to the last. A Wild Hunt ends only with the death of either the sworn foe or the pack sent to bring it down.

Attachment [Wolves of Orboros] – This attachment can be added to a Wolves of Orboros unit.

CHIEFTAIN

⚔ **Combined Melee Attack**

≋ **Officer**

🌙 **Pathfinder**

Power Swell – Once per game during its unit's activation, this model can use Power Swell. During this activation, models in this unit gain an additional die on melee damage rolls.

Tactics: Ranked Attacks – Models in this unit gain Ranked Attacks. (Friendly Faction models can ignore models with Ranked Attacks when determining LOS.)

STANDARD BEARER

🌙 **Pathfinder**

🚩 **Standard Bearer**

CLEFT SPEAR

⚔ **Reach**

Powerful Charge – This model gains +2 to charge attack rolls with this weapon.

CHIEFTAIN						
SPD	STR	MAT	RAT	DEF	ARM	CMD
6	5	7	4	13	13	8

CLEFT SPEAR		
	POW	P+S
	4	9

STANDARD BEARER						
SPD	STR	MAT	RAT	DEF	ARM	CMD
6	5	6	4	13	13	8

CHIEFTAIN'S DAMAGE	5
FIELD ALLOWANCE	1
CHIEFTAIN & STANDARD BEARER	2
SMALL BASE	

A master of the hunt never speaks his name, his identity subsumed by the pack. These skilled killers have touched the essence of wildness and conducted many kills. A feral madness fills their eyes and a coarse timbre tinges their voices. Such masters work their Wolves into a state of fevered expectation and barely contained bloodlust so that when they finally attack, they are men no longer. Fighting as wild beasts wielding spears as fangs and executing fluid movements with unspoken coordination, all Wolves are perfectly aware of their place within the pack.

BLACKCLAD WAYFARER
CIRCLE SOLO

Thunder and lightning shall mark the time for you to strike.

—Conor Deorain, wayfarer

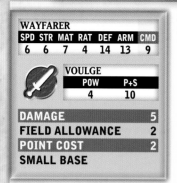

WAYFARER						
SPD	STR	MAT	RAT	DEF	ARM	CMD
6	6	7	4	14	13	9

VOULGE		
	POW	P+S
	4	10

DAMAGE	5
FIELD ALLOWANCE	2
POINT COST	2
SMALL BASE	

WAYFARER

- ⊛ **Commander**
- ⊘ **Immunity: Cold**
- ⊘ **Immunity: Electricity**
- ⊘ **Immunity: Fire**
- ☾ **Pathfinder**

Magic Ability [7]

- **Hunter's Mark (★Attack)** – Hunter's Mark is a RNG 10 magic attack that causes no damage. Friendly models can charge or make a slam power attack against an enemy model hit by Hunter's Mark without being forced or spending focus. A friendly model charging an enemy model hit by Hunter's Mark gains +2" of movement. Hunter's Mark lasts for one turn.

- **Phase Jump (★Action)** – If it is within 2" of a friendly Shifting Stone model, place this model anywhere completely within 12" of its current location. Otherwise, place it within 2" of a friendly Shifting Stone model anywhere on the table. After using Phase Jump, this model's activation ends.

- **Stone Spray (★Attack)** – Stone Spray is a RNG SP 8, POW 12 magic attack. On a critical hit, the model hit is knocked down.

VOULGE

- ⊘ **Magical Weapon**
- ⊘ **Reach**

TACTICAL TIPS

MAGIC ABILITY – Performing a Magic Ability special action or special attack counts as casting a spell.

HUNTER'S MARK – Modifiers to movement apply only to a model's normal movement.

Shifting stones pulse with strange light as a wayfarer steps near, for he boasts a special connection to these stones and their power to move man or beast along the thrumming ley lines below the surface of the earth. Druids gathered in secret at their far-flung sacred sites can expect a wayfarer to appear at any time bearing news of key struggles or omens of conflicts to come. Wayfarers bearing the seal of the omnipotents arrive to pass down orders and conscribe subordinate druids and their allies to war.

A wayfarer enters battle with the confidence of decades spent honing his power. His arrival throws enemies into chaos as they scramble to deal with the unexpected threat. In an instant he vanishes with a thunderclap only to reappear amid his allies to lead them to victory.

With a peal of thunder and the scent of ozone, a wayfarer appears deep behind enemy lines. Moving unseen, wind swirling around his black-cowled form, he raises his hands to the darkening heavens. Clouds heavy with storm buckle and heave at his summons. While the enemy hesitates in fear and confusion, howls emerge from the darkness as the druid's allies pour forth from the trees with terrible swiftness to answer his call.

DRUID WILDER
CIRCLE SOLO

Each wilder has the potential for greatness, just as the quiet eddy can become a great storm.
—Kaya the Moonhunter

TACTICAL TIPS

ATTACHED – This model cannot be reassigned if its warcaster is destroyed or removed from play.

Every blackclad is a potent invoker of the world's primal energies; even the least commands the fundamental powers of nature and chaos. But the journey to true power is long, and a druid must first serve before being deemed ready to command. Young druids learn the ways of the order through a lengthy apprenticeship, gaining knowledge from observation as much as from instruction. The most promising wilders accompany their masters into battle, where they learn to command ferocious warbeasts and channel their druidic powers in combat.

This stage of initiation into the Circle's mysteries is extremely dangerous. Wilders are expected to serve as their master's right hands and obey without question. Though few warlocks will expend the life of a wilder casually, the young druids often find themselves in harm's way. Those

WILDER

⬡ Pathfinder

Attached – Before the start of the game, attach this model to a friendly Faction warlock for the rest of the game. Each warlock can have only one model attached to it.

Herding – While this model is in its warlock's control area, the warlock can force, leach, reave, heal, and transfer damage to the warbeasts in its battlegroup that are in this model's command range.

Magic Ability [6]

- **Condition (★Action)** – RNG 3. Target friendly Faction warbeast. If the warbeast is in range, place any number of fury points on or remove any number of fury points from it.

- **Spirit Tap (★Action)** – This model immediately casts the animus of a friendly Faction warbeast in its command range as a spell. This model cannot cast an animus with a RNG of SELF. This model must make a special attack to cast an offensive spell. Other spells are cast by making a special action.

STAFF

⬡ Magical Weapon

⬡ Reach

WILDER						
SPD	STR	MAT	RAT	DEF	ARM	CMD
6	5	5	4	14	11	7

STAFF		
	POW	P+S
	3	8

DAMAGE	5
FIELD ALLOWANCE	1
POINT COST	2
SMALL BASE	

who survive their years of training emerge from the crucible stronger, ready to take their place as warlocks in their own right.

REEVE HUNTER
CIRCLE REEVE OF OROBOROS SOLO

It is a poor hunter who lies in wait for his prey to stumble across his path. Far better to seek out your quarry and bring it down on the run.

—Hunter Karin Telmos

HUNTER						
SPD	STR	MAT	RAT	DEF	ARM	CMD
6	6	6	7	13	13	8

DOUBLE CROSSBOW			
RNG	ROF	AOE	POW
12	1	—	10

BATTLE BLADE	
POW	P+S
3	9

CLEFT SWORD	
POW	P+S
5	11

DAMAGE	5
FIELD ALLOWANCE	2
POINT COST	2

SMALL BASE

HUNTER

⬤ Pathfinder

Camouflage – This model gains an additional +2 DEF when benefiting from concealment or cover.

Hunter – This model ignores forests, concealment, and cover when determining LOS or making a ranged attack.

Leadership [Reeves of Oroboros] – While in this model's command range, friendly Reeves of Oroboros models gain Camouflage.

Quick Work – When this model destroys one or more enemy models with a melee attack during its combat action, immediately after that attack is resolved this model can make one normal ranged attack. Attacks gained from Quick Work do not count against a weapon's ROF.

Snap Fire – When this model destroys one or more enemy models with a ranged attack during its combat action, immediately after that attack is resolved this model can make one normal ranged attack. Attacks gained from Snap Fire do not count against a weapon's ROF and cannot generate additional attacks from Snap Fire.

Swift Hunter – When this model destroys an enemy model with a normal ranged attack, immediately after the attack is resolved it can advance up to 2″.

CLEFT SWORD

Powerful Charge – This model gains +2 to charge attack rolls with this weapon.

TACTICAL TIPS

CAMOUFLAGE – If a model ignores concealment or cover, it also ignores concealment or cover's Camouflage bonus.

QUICK WORK – This model cannot make the additional attack if it is still in melee.

they are hunting denizens of the deep woods, they are no less adept at hunting men. Years of service alongside their fellow reeves have honed their skills to a razor's edge, and they strike with murderous acuity on the battlefield.

When the blackclads muster the reeves to war, they look to the greatest hunters among them to be their advance scouts and assassins. Such is the hunters' skill in woodcraft that they can move undetected across the most barren terrain and disappear as if into shadows even under the midday sun. While they can remain still when stalking prey, reeves are experts at evasion and the art of positioning, and once they attack they are always in motion. They barely pause to mark their targets before letting loose a flurry of precisely aimed bolts and moving on to find their next quarry.

Many reeves die at a young age, cut down in battle or torn to pieces by the claws and fangs of savage forest creatures. Those who survive become legends among their kind, able to track great beasts to their lairs by following them for miles without being detected. Demonstrating incredible patience, hunters follow in stealth and wait for the right moment to bring their dangerous prey low with just a few carefully aimed bolts. As skilled as

THARN RAVAGER WHITE MANE
CIRCLE SOLO

You are proud of your scars, of the few times you have tasted your prey's heart. Return to me when your axe-brides are beyond counting.
—Morikai, white mane of the Kival tuath

TACTICAL TIPS

TACTICIAN – This includes this model.

The lives of the Tharn are difficult, and most of their warriors die young in battle. Those few veterans who survive decades of hunts and overcome the odds to reach their senior years become white manes, seasoned killers their younger kin look to with both respect and fear. These eldest Tharn think nothing of taking life beyond the brutal joy they derive from the act and the vigor they gain from the life essence of their prey. Having grown strong on the blood and hearts of their victims for most of their lives, white manes are the embodiment of Tharn in their prime. Even without the reflexes of youth they are utterly deadly, having mastered their weapons and gained instincts for battle that verge on supernatural.

White manes do not fear death; rather, they look forward to dying gloriously on the battlefield, knee-deep in the blood and entrails of their foes. These warriors prefer a final blaze of savagery to the quiet fading of old age. Seeing such a

WHITE MANE

✠ **Fearless**

🐾 **Pathfinder**

Heart Eater – This model gains a corpse token each time it destroys a living enemy model with a melee attack. This model can have up to three corpse tokens at a time. It can spend corpse tokens during its activation to boost an attack or damage roll or to make an additional melee attack at one token per boost or additional attack.

Overtake – When this model destroys one or more enemy warrior models with a normal melee attack, after the attack is resolved this model can immediately advance up to 1".

Sprint – At the end of this model's activation, if it destroyed one or more enemy models with melee attacks this activation it can make a full advance.

Tactician [Tharn Ravager] – While in this model's command range, friendly Tharn Ravager models ignore other friendly Tharn Ravager models when determining LOS. Friendly Tharn Ravager models can advance through other friendly Tharn Ravager models in this model's command range without effect if they have enough movement to move completely past them.

Treewalker – This model ignores forests when determining LOS. While in a forest, this model gains +2 DEF against melee attack rolls and can advance through obstructions and other models if it has enough movement to move completely past them.

THARN AXE

⟳ **Reach**

Powerful Charge – This model gains +2 to charge attack rolls with this weapon.

WHITE MANE						
SPD	STR	MAT	RAT	DEF	ARM	CMD
6	8	8	3	13	14	8

THARN AXE	
POW	P+S
5	13

DAMAGE	8
FIELD ALLOWANCE	2
POINT COST	3
MEDIUM BASE	

veteran charge into battle inspires ravagers to a frenzied state as they rush to follow his example. A white mane's scarred countenance and grisly tokens proudly mark countless kills and many years of brutal fighting.

WAR WOLF
CIRCLE SOLO

Others tremble at the howl of a wolf in the darkness. To us it means a brother returns home.

—Kund, Wolves of Orboros huntsman

WAR WOLF						
SPD	STR	MAT	RAT	DEF	ARM	CMD
7	7	6	0	13	12	7

BITE		
	POW	P+S
	4	11

DAMAGE	5
FIELD ALLOWANCE	**3**
POINT COST	**1**
MEDIUM BASE	

WAR WOLF

⊙ **Pathfinder**

Gang Fighter – When making a melee attack targeting an enemy model in melee range of another friendly Faction warrior model, this model gains +2 to melee attack and melee damage rolls.

Hunter – This model ignores forests, concealment, and cover when determining LOS or making a ranged attack.

Sic 'Em [Reeve of Orboros] – Once per turn if this model is not in melee, when a friendly Reeve of Orboros hits an enemy model with an attack, immediately after the attack is resolved this model can charge the model hit. This model's charge attack roll is boosted.

The Wolves of Orboros consider themselves kin of their namesake. This attitude literally extends to fighting side-by-side with half-wild animals and speaking of them as brothers. The hulking beasts kept by the Wolves are of stocky mountain breeds found in northern Khador and among the Cygnaran Wyrmwall Mountains. They bring speed, exceptional senses, and raw killing power as their natural assets.

The breeds chosen by these warriors do not behave as their wilder kin do, but neither are they tamed hounds bred for war. They are something in-between. Tales passed down through the older families of the Wolves of Orboros describe the animals hunting alongside mountain men of ancient Molgur tribes. Perhaps there was some compact made between the ancestors of these men and wolves that bound them together. For reasons not well understood, the wolves immediately recognize the scent of these scions and seek them out. The animals offer themselves to their allies fully, not even begrudging the warriors their pelts.

War wolves do not respond to shouted commands but instead fight on their own initiative. They are cunning creatures, however, and do not need to be told to lie in wait until the spears of the Wolves have pinned an enemy in place. They circle at the ready and move from behind to take the enemy unaware. At the distinctive sound of the reeves' crossbows they leap from the trees as a blur of ghostly fur, their fangs bared to tear into tendons and muscle.

We called the Lord of the Feast to slaughter in the time of the Orgoth. He stalked those places stolen from us and littered the forest floor with the bones of our enemies.
—Omnipotent Dahlekov

TACTICAL TIPS

BLOOD REAPER – The melee attacks are all simultaneous.

SHIFTER – This attack causes no damage.

A walking horror of prehistory, the Lord of the Feast feeds the ravenous hunger of the Devourer Wurm. It lurks in shadow and falls upon those doomed to cross its path. From each victim the Feast Lord claims the viscera and vital organs. It then prepares its sacrificial offering to the Beast of All Shapes and is rewarded with a wave of savage power. Upon the completion of its work, the Lord of the Feast transforms into ravens that linger to consume the eyes of the slain.

The Circle seldom intentionally draws the attention of the Devourer, for they prefer to tap into the mindless power

LORD OF THE FEAST

- **Advance Deployment**
- **Fearless**
- **Pathfinder**
- **Stealth**
- **Terror**

Blood Reaper – When this model makes its first melee attack during its activation, it makes one melee attack with this weapon against each model in its LOS and this weapon's melee range.

Heart Eater – This model gains a corpse token each time it destroys a living enemy model with a melee attack. This model can have up to three corpse tokens at a time. It can spend corpse tokens during its activation to boost an attack or damage roll or to make an additional melee attack at one token per boost or additional attack.

Virtuoso – This model can make melee and ranged attacks during the same combat action. When this model makes its initial attacks, it can make both its initial ranged and melee attacks.

RAVEN

Shifter – When this attack hits an enemy model, immediately after the attack is resolved place this model B2B with the enemy model.

WURMBLADE

- **Magical Weapon**
- **Reach**

LORD OF THE FEAST						
SPD	STR	MAT	RAT	DEF	ARM	CMD
5	8	8	7	12	17	10

RAVEN			
RNG	ROF	AOE	POW
10	1	—	—

WURMBLADE	
POW	P+S
5	13

DAMAGE	8
FIELD ALLOWANCE	C
POINT COST	4
SMALL BASE	

of Orboros that suffuses the world. Dark times sometimes require dark measures, however, and the druids have begun to call upon the forgotten lore once known only to the highest priests of the Molgur tribes. With these black rites they have once again summoned an avatar of the Unsleeping One and unleashed it upon the living.

The Lord of the Feast's only companion is a raven that ranges ahead of its master, leading its lord to fresh victims. Emerging like a shadow of death, the Feast Lord whirls its long blade in a storm of steel, carving into enemy flesh as it relishes its banquet of bloody sacrifice.

WOLF LORD MORRAIG
CIRCLE LIGHT CAVALRY DRAGOON CHARACTER SOLO

Even as a babe Morraig bore his enemies' blood, in the fire of his hair.

—Morvahna the Autumnblade

MORRAIG						
SPD	STR	MAT	RAT	DEF	ARM	CMD
8/6	7	8	4	14	17/15	9

CLEFT BLADE

POW	P+S
6	13

MOUNT

POW
12

MOUNTED DAMAGE	10
DISMOUNTED DAMAGE	5
FIELD ALLOWANCE	C
POINT COST	5
LARGE BASE MOUNTED	
SMALL BASE DISMOUNTED	

MORRAIG

- ✪ Commander
- ✠ Fearless
- ☾ Pathfinder

Cleave – When this model destroys one or more enemy models with a melee attack during its activation, immediately after the attack is resolved the model can make one additional melee attack. This model can gain only one additional attack from Cleave each activation.

Dragoon – While mounted, this model has base SPD 8 and base ARM 17. While dismounted, it has base SPD 6, base ARM 15.

Flank [Wolves of Orboros] – When this model makes a melee attack against an enemy model within the melee range of a friendly model of the type indicated, this model gains +2 to attack rolls and gains an additional damage die.

Prowl – This model gains Stealth ⚑ while within terrain that provides concealment, the AOE of a spell that provides concealment, or the AOE of a cloud effect.

CLEFT BLADE

- ⟳ Reach
- ⚔ Weapon Master

Morraig was born in the accursed Vescheneg Headlands of western Khador, but his stock derives from the Wyrmwall Mountains. His people trace their ancestry back to the Molgur, and they have ever served the Circle Orboros. They have uprooted themselves and moved where needed countless times, spreading their progeny across the entire region; sometimes he jokes that any wilderness man with a touch of flame in his hair is likely a kinsman. Few among the Wolves of Orboros do not recognize him. Elders treat him like a long-lost son, those of fighting years embrace him as a brother, and the young wish their fathers were more like him.

Certainly Morraig has done more to expand the ranks of the Wolves of Orboros than any dozen of his peers. When he enters a snowed-in hunter's lodge and shares drinks and stories, invariably half the able-bodied men present will put aside old aspirations to join his brotherhood. Though he claims the talk of destiny is nonsense, he seems to be working hard to prepare the Wolves for some coming conflict.

The companionable demeanor he bears when gathered around the fire with his brothers in arms contrasts with the utter ferocity and ruthlessness he embodies in war. He trains his men until they can no longer stand, often forcing them to march through forests in the dead of night as rain pours down upon their heads. He is an uncompromising master, but those who follow him know he forges them into burnished weapons and take inspiration from seeing him lead the charge against the enemies of Orboros. Few can match his cleft sword, and the enraged wolf beneath him snaps at any who evade his blade's edge. The unusual motion of his steed has proven to be an advantage against more than one adversary expecting to face a horseman's charge. Those thinking themselves his equal are often disabused of the notion upon feeling his blade thrust through their breastplates.

The Wolf Lord has long been obedient to the druids, but in recent years he has come to view no man his master and only a few blackclads worthy of his respect. His ultimate fidelity is to the men he leads, yet on some instinctive level he knows he marches toward some larger purpose. When Morraig first met Krueger the Stormlord, a thrill of recognition shot through him. As he clasped hands with

Every age sees those few who enter the world an embodiment of ancient ancestors, equipped with instincts and dispositions setting them apart from other of their era. They may remember places and events forgotten by the living and never recorded, through dreams or impressions when they walk the places where their ancestors left an indelible mark. Morraig is such a man, the inheritor of an ancient and proud bloodline that seems to guide him toward some greater reckoning with the past.

Even among the most respected elder huntsmen of the Wolves of Orboros, Morraig seems larger than life, a man whose voice crackles with the thunder of command. War wolves, who barely tolerate the touch of man, gladly bear him into battle and fight to the death to defend him.

Morraig is a pragmatic warrior predestined to lead men into war. He feels little tolerance for mystical talk, shifting uncomfortably in his saddle when blackclads scheme and invoke their magic. He has become used to such sights as the warlord of nearly a third of the Wolves of Orboros in western Immoren, but his mind remains rooted in practical matters.

the arrogant druid something beyond words connected in their stares. Morraig took his men into the service of the Stormlord even as emissaries from other potents sent polite but increasingly agitated queries. Whether he and Krueger journey to glory or to ruin, Morraig has made his choice, and where he marches an army of the Wolves of Orboros follows.

PAINTING CIRCLE ORBOROS

The color scheme of the Circle Orboros incorporates the most natural tones of any HORDES faction. Various greens, browns, earthy greys, and black harmonize to create a wild and earthy look. The scheme achieves contrast by balancing warm browns, bronze, and flesh with cool black, grey stone, and cool green tones. Much of the contrast is achieved through differences in value, such as when dark green nests within shining bronze or a green glow spills from cracked stone. When painting a scheme of natural colors such as this one, pay particularly close attention to the value contrast. This will help you avoid an army that from afar appears muddy or is hard for the eye to interpret.

PAINTING TERMINOLOGY

BASECOAT
The initial coat of paint on which everything else will be built. It is important that the basecoat is very clean and every color is where it should be. Your shades and highlights will coordinate with the basecoat and main color choices.

DRYBRUSHING
The quick way to highlight a textured surface. Use a lighter color, but remove most of the paint from your brush by stroking the bristles on a paper towel until the paint is almost gone. Then carefully and quickly move the brush back and forth across the surface of the miniature.

GLAZE
A mixture of water and a small amount of ink that is applied in successive layers to subtly tint an area.

HIGHLIGHTING
A lighter color applied to the basecoat in the raised areas of a miniature to create the look of light hitting the surface. When highlighting in multiple steps, keep a little bit of the underlying color showing, overlapping them like the shingles on a roof.

SHADING
A darker color applied to the basecoat in the recessed areas of a miniature to create shadows. Exaggerating the shade and highlight colors will add to the visual appeal of a model.

WASH
A tinted mix liberally applied to the basecoat to create detailed shading. The wash will run into the smallest crevasses on a model and dry as a shadow, so it needs to be a darker color than the basecoat. The wash mix works well as **4** parts mixing medium, **1** part paint/ink, and **3** parts water.

FEMALE FLESH

Step 1) Basecoat with a 50/50 mix of Midlund Flesh and Ryn Flesh.

Step 2) For the initial shading, use Midlund Flesh mixed with Battledress Green and some mixing medium for translucency. Apply as soft shadows.

Step 3) Mix Midlund Flesh, Skorne Red, and mixing medium for the final shading. For a feminine look, avoid accentuating the paranasal cleft (the crease in the upper lip) and make sure there are no hard lines when you are done.

Step 4) Highlight with a 50/50 mix of Ryn Flesh and mixing medium. The mixing medium will help keep the transitions smooth and the overall look silky soft.

☐ **Midlund Flesh**   ☐ **Battledress Green**

☐ **Ryn Flesh**   ☐ **Skorne Red**

THARN FLESH

Step 1) Basecoat the flesh with a mixture of Midlund Flesh and Gun Corps Brown.

Step 2) Add Skorne Red to the previous mixture and use this to apply shading.

Step 3) Add Battledress Green and Thornwood Green to the previous mixture and use this for the final shading.

Step 4) Begin highlighting with a mixture of Gun Corps Brown and Ryn Flesh

Step 5) Apply final highlights using Ryn Flesh.

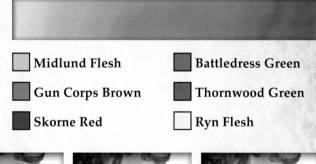

☐ **Midlund Flesh**   ☐ **Battledress Green**

☐ **Gun Corps Brown**   ☐ **Thornwood Green**

☐ **Skorne Red**   ☐ **Ryn Flesh**

BEAST FLESH

Step 1) Basecoat the skin and fur with a mix of Trollblood Highlight, Menoth White Highlight, and Hammerfall Khaki.

Step 2) Blend a mix of Beast Hide and Hammerfall Khaki into the skin areas that will become darker, like the hip area. Wash the fur near the hoof with a mix of Trollblood Highlight, Battlefield Brown, and mixing medium.

Step 3) Add Gun Corps Brown and Bloodtracker Brown to the skin mix, and blend it onto the skin. As the blending steps get darker, paint less and less surface area so the color shifts transition well. Blend pure Battlefield Brown into the bottom area of the fur.

Step 4) Continue blending the skin, this time using pure Bloodstone. Paint the tips of the fur area with thinned Thamar Black.

Step 5) To complete the skin, shade under the muscles with a mix of Ironhull Grey, Menoth White Highlight, and Hammerfall Khaki. Follow with a final blend of Exile Blue and Battlefield Brown.

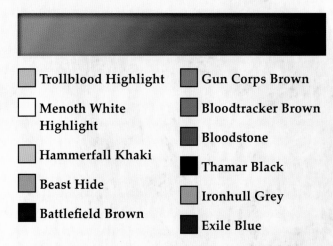

- ☐ Trollblood Highlight
- ☐ Menoth White Highlight
- ☐ Hammerfall Khaki
- ☐ Beast Hide
- ☐ Battlefield Brown
- ☐ Gun Corps Brown
- ☐ Bloodtracker Brown
- ☐ Bloodstone
- ☐ Thamar Black
- ☐ Ironhull Grey
- ☐ Exile Blue

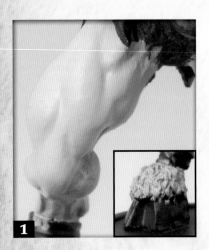

1

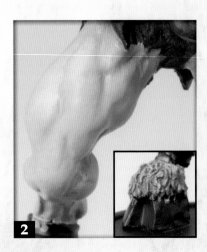

2

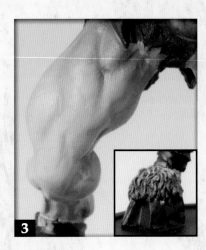

3

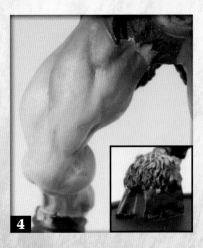

4

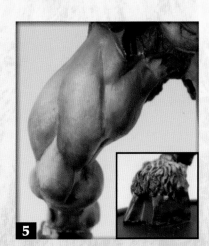

5

PATTERNED CLOTH

Step 1) Basecoat the cloth with Ironhull Grey, then paint the lightning bolt pattern using Trollblood Highlight. Use Cryx Bane Highlight to basecoat the fur lining.

Step 2) To give the impression the lines in the pattern overlap, follow the course of a line using Ironhull Grey. You can also clean up the pattern as you go to save time. Next, give the fur lining a wash of Thornwood Green mixed with Beast Hide. Trace a line of Umbral Umber mixed with Thamar Black along the edges of the cloak where the fur meets the cloth to separate the areas.

Step 3) To shade the cloth, mix Idrian Flesh, Exile Blue, and a small dot of Thamar Black. Apply this mix to the folds of the cloak, and while it is still wet, use a second brush to blend it over the basecoat. This method shades the basecoat and the pattern simultaneously. For the fur, take 'Jack Bone and apply it using the side of your brush to paint multiple strands of fur at once. If this is done correctly the paint should stay out of the crevices.

Step 4) Mix Ironhull Grey with Morrow White and highlight the hood and edges of the cloak but not the folds. For the pattern highlights, mix

some Trollblood Highlight with Menoth White Highlight. Using a fine tip brush, trace a fine line along the top of each bolt so they appear to catch the light. Highlight the fur with Menoth White Highlight applied the same way as in step 3 but isolating only the tops of each fold.

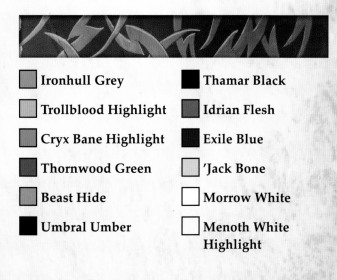

⬜ Ironhull Grey	⬛ Thamar Black
⬜ Trollblood Highlight	⬛ Idrian Flesh
⬜ Cryx Bane Highlight	⬛ Exile Blue
⬜ Thornwood Green	⬜ 'Jack Bone
⬜ Beast Hide	⬜ Morrow White
⬛ Umbral Umber	⬜ Menoth White Highlight

CREATING DRUID LATTICE PATTERNS

To recreate the patterns found on Circle Orboros garments, first create radiating arcs from a central point as illustrated here in black. Then intersect the arcs with randomly positioned hook shapes, illustrated here in grey.

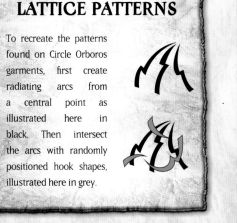

LACQUERED BRONZE

Step 1) Begin with a basecoat of Molten Bronze mixed with a touch of Umbral Umber and thinned with a little Brown Ink and water.

Step 2) Wash the inner recessed areas with a mix of Meredius Blue, Iosan Green, mixing medium, and water.

Step 3) Paint thin shadow lines under the raised bronze areas with Coal Black. Paint the undersides only. Imagine a light is shining above the model and you're painting in the shadows under the raised sections.

Step 4) Glaze the recessed areas with Turquoise Ink. To avoid leaving pools of watery paint, use just enough in a thin layer to tint the area. Apply multiple coats to get the desired effect.

Step 5) Blend Molten Bronze onto the central raised portions of the lacquered areas for translucency. Highlight the bronze trim with Molten Bronze and clean up any messes caused when creating the lacquered look.

Step 6) Use Brown Ink to glaze the lacquered areas that would have a shadow cast on them from the raised bronze areas.

Step 7) Highlight the bronze with a mix of Rhulic Gold and Brass Balls.

Step 8) Apply a final highlight to the upper edges of the bronze with a mix of Brass Balls and Radiant Platinum.

▢ Molten Bronze		▢ Coal Black
■ Umbral Umber		▢ Turquoise Ink
▢ Brown Ink		▢ Rhulic Gold
▢ Meredius Blue		▢ Brass Balls
▢ Iosan Green		▢ Radiant Platinum

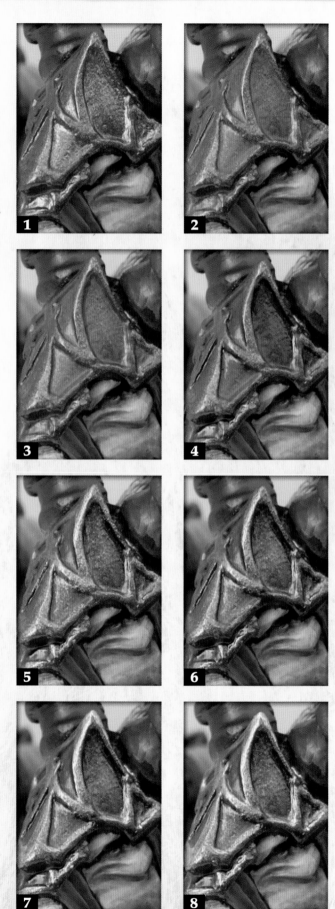

STONE

Step 1) Basecoat the stone with Bastion Grey.

Step 2) Use an old brush to spatter the surface with colors such as Thamar Black, Menoth White Highlight, and Underbelly Blue.

Step 3) Apply shading using a mixture of Greatcoat Grey and Thornwood Green plus a few drops of mixing medium for translucency.

Step 4) Highlight with a mix of Trollblood Highlight, Menoth White Highlight, and mixing medium.

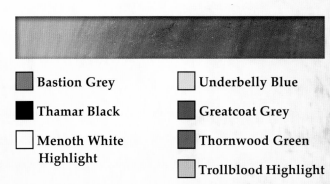

- Bastion Grey
- Thamar Black
- Menoth White Highlight
- Underbelly Blue
- Greatcoat Grey
- Thornwood Green
- Trollblood Highlight

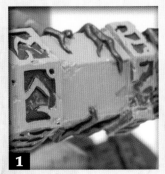
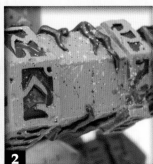
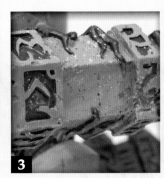

GREEN GLOW

Step 1) Using watered-down Menoth White Highlight, allow the paint to flow into the areas you wish to glow.

Step 2) Repeat step 1 with a mixture of Wurm Green plus one drop of Yellow Ink and a few drops of mixing medium and water.

Step 3) Apply a glaze of Green Ink to the areas where the glow is least concentrated.

Step 4) Add Menoth White Highlight to the mixture from step 2. Use a fine-tip brush to dab this color into the corners and cracks, letting capillary action carry the paint into the recesses.

- Menoth White Highlight
- Wurm Green
- Yellow Ink
- Green Ink

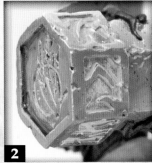

CIRCLE GALLERY

KAYA THE WILDBORNE
Warlock

KAYA THE MOONHUNTER & LARIS
Warlock & Light Warbeast

KRUEGER THE STORMWRATH
Warlock

KRUEGER THE STORMLORD
Warlock

BALDUR THE STONECLEAVER
Warlock

MORVAHNA THE AUTUMNBLADE
Warlock

MOHSAR THE DESERTWALKER
Warlock

CASSIUS THE OATHKEEPER & WURMWOOD, TREE OF FATE
Warlock & Solo

KROMAC THE RAVENOUS
Warlock & Beast Form

DRUID OF ORBOROS OVERSEER
Unit Attachment

BLACKCLAD WAYFARER
Solo

WOLDWYRD
Light Warbeast

MEGALITH
Heavy Warbeast

WOLDWATCHER
Light Warbeast

DRUIDS OF ORBOROS
Unit

WOLDWARDEN
Heavy Warbeast

FERAL WARPWOLF
Heavy Warbeast

STONE KEEPER
Unit Attachment

SHIFTING STONES
Unit

WARPBORN SKINWALKERS
Unit

STONEWARD & WOLDSTALKERS
Unit

WOLD GUARDIAN
Heavy Warbeast

PUREBLOOD WARPWOLF
Heavy Warbeast

WARPWOLF STALKER
Heavy Warbeast

WOLVES OF ORBOROS
Unit

WOLVES OF ORBOROS OFFICER & TOTEM BEARER
Unit Attachment

ARGUS
Light Warbeast

SENTRY STONE & MANNIKINS
Solos

REEVES OF ORBOROS
Unit

GORAX
Light Warbeast

REEVE OF ORBOROS CHIEFTAIN & STANDARD
Unit Attachment

WOLF LORD MORRAIG
Dragoon Solo

WAR WOLF
Solo

THARN RAVAGERS
Unit

THARN RAVAGER SHAMAN
Unit Attachment

THARN RAVAGER WHITE MANE
Solo

THARN BLOODWEAVERS
Unit

SHADOWHORN SATYR
Heavy Warbeast

GNARLHORN SATYR
Heavy Warbeast

THARN WOLF RIDERS
Unit

LORD OF THE FEAST
Solo

WARPWOLF EXTREME
Heavy Warbeast

DRUID WILDER
Solo

THARN BLOODTRACKERS
Unit